MAIN TRENDS IN MODERN LINGUISTICS

MAIN TRENDS IN MODERN LINGUISTICS

MAURICE LEROY
Professor of Linguistics in the University of Brussels

Translated by
GLANVILLE PRICE
Professor of French in the University of Stirling

UNIVERSITY OF CALIFORNIA PRESS
BERKELEY AND LOS ANGELES
1967

University of California Press
Berkeley and Los Angeles, California

© *in this translation Basil Blackwell 1967*

This is a translation of *Les Grands Courants
de la Linguistique Moderne*, published by
Presses Universitaires de Bruxelles and
Presses Universitaires de France in
conjunction in 1963.

Library of Congress Catalog Card Number: 67–13140

Printed in Great Britain

Contents

PART TWO

Preface

THE aim of this book is to give a concise general survey of the main trends in modern linguistics rather than a detailed chronological account of all the ups and downs of its development. We have tried to highlight the outstanding events in the history of linguistics and sift out from the whole body of research the main underlying ideas that have provoked fruitful discussion and given a new stamp to contemporary thinking. If we have neglected details—and anyone who wishes to do so can easily obtain further information on points of particular interest elsewhere—we nevertheless believe we have not left out anything essential to an awareness of problems of language. If we have particularly stressed questions of method and the principles that have guided research, the reason is that we have had constantly in mind the thought that this is a fundamental part of a young linguist's training and that no recent manual on these lines is as yet available. Bertil Malmberg's excellent and original survey, *Nya vägar inom språkforskningen: En orientering i modern lingvistik*, Stockholm, 1959, is written in Swedish and therefore not as widely known as it deserves to be;[1] Louis Kukenheim's *Esquisse historique de la linguistique française et de ses rapports avec la linguistique générale*, Leiden, 1962, is precise and detailed, and has a wealth of bibliographical indications but it is primarily and intentionally concerned specifically with French linguistics; and the collective volume, *Trends in European and American Linguistics, 1930–1960*, edited on the occasion of the Ninth International Congress of Linguists by Christine Mohrmann, Alf Sommerfelt and J. Whatmough, Utrecht-Antwerp, 1961, deals only—and unevenly—with certain selected problems.[2]

[1] This book has now been translated into English by E. Carney under the title *New Trends in Linguistics*, Stockholm-Lund, 1964 (=*Bibliotheca Linguistica*, Vol. I).

[2] [The English translation by Muriel Heppell of Milka Ivić's *Trends in Linguistics*, The Hague, 1965 (= *Janua Linguarum*, Series minor, XLII), of which the Serbo-Croatian original was published in 1963, appeared as the present translation was about to go to press.]

It may be thought that we have devoted too much attention to the technical side of linguistics—i.e. comparative and historical grammar—whereas we ought to have concentrated on general linguistics proper, i.e. on reflection upon language and its different manifestations. But we are convinced that the two aspects are intimately linked and condition one another: it was the development and perfecting of comparative grammar that made it possible to draw up general theories and, inversely, general linguistics has stimulated new methods of investigation on the technical plane of comparison in both the synchronic and the diachronic dimensions.

As our aim has not been to produce a work of erudition references have been kept to a minimum. However, such brief indications as are given will enable the reader to compile a bibliography for any aspect he wishes to study further.

We do not for a moment think we have covered everything. What after all do we mean by linguistics? What are its limits? Some kinds of research relate to two or more branches of study or can be envisaged from two or more viewpoints. In the human sciences, of which linguistics is one, we are in the realm of the continuous and any attempt to set up water-tight compartments is doomed to failure, except perhaps as a convenient way of presenting the facts didactically. This explains why we have avoided a rigid division into chapters and paragraphs, with the hope that any disadvantage of this method may be compensated for by frequent cross-references and by the index. The reason for the plan adopted, for dividing the book into three parts, will become clear to anyone who reads straight through the book. We shall discuss this further in the Conclusion. If we seem to stress some schools of thought or some theories more than others, this may be because we consider them to represent particularly important trends in linguistic thinking or perhaps indeed because we ourself sympathize with their point of view: anyone who dares to pass judgment on his own times is inevitably influenced to some extent by subjective factors.

It may be thought that we have devoted more attention to Indo-European than its position amongst the languages of the world justifies. However, quite apart from the fact that the author, who is an Indo-Europeanist, has not wished to go beyond the bounds of his own competence, it is on the basis of the comparative grammar of the Indo-European languages that the scientific method of modern linguistics has been patiently built up.

During these last few years, we have published a number of articles dealing with some of the problems discussed in this book, and have drawn on them when writing the book. In order not to overload the text with notes, we mention the fact now, once and for all, and list here the articles in question:

'Sur le concept d'évolution en linguistique', in *Revue de l'Institut de Sociologie*, 1949, 337–375.

'Tendances au doctrinarisme dans la pensée linguistique contemporaine', in *Mélanges Georges Smets*, Brussels, 1952, pp. 523–532.

'Benedetto Croce et les études linguistiques', in *Revue Internationale de Philosophie*, VII (1953), 342–362.

'Orientamenti attuali della linguistica generale', in *Atti del II Convegno Internazionale di Linguisti*, Milan, 1953, pp. 1–14.

'Le social et l'individuel dans la science du language', in *Revue de l'Institut de Sociologie*, 1953, 475–489.

'Aspects récents de la linguistique indo-européenne', in *Phoibos*, VIII–IX (1953–1955), 23–35.

'Les langues du monde et la typologie linguistique', in *Mémoires et Publications de la Société des Sciences, des Arts et des Lettres du Hainaut*, LXXIV (1960), 169–204.

'Über den heutigen Stand der Sprachwissenschaft', in *Das Altertum*, VI (1960), 195–204.

'Stratificazioni cronologiche nei rapporti fra le lingue indeuropee', in *Indeuropeo e Protostoria. Atti del III Convegno Internazionale di Linguisti*, Milan, 1961, pp. 63–79.

'Le renouveau de la sémantique', in *Innsbrucker Beiträge zur Kulturwissenschaft*, Sonderheft 15 (=*II. Fachtagung für indogermanische und allgemeine Sprachwissenschaft*), Innsbruck, 1962, pp. 95–106.

'La classification en linguistique', in *La classification dans les sciences*, Gembloux, 1963, pp. 132–154.

Author's Note to the English Edition

Le manuscrit de l'édition française avait bénéficié des remarques de mes Collègues Ér. Buyssens, Alb. Henry, L. Rocher et Ad. Van Loey ainsi que de l'aide de Mme R. Rocher pour la confection des index. Le texte de la présente version anglaise a été établi par notre Collègue de l'Université de Stirling, M. Glanville Price, qui n'a pas manqué de suggérer d'utiles améliorations pour lesquelles nous le remercions vivement; nous avons en outre tenu compte dans une certaine mesure de la bibliographie récente, des quelques corrections apportées à la version italienne (qui a paru à Bari, chez Laterza, en 1965 sous le titre *Profilo storico della linguistica moderna*) ainsi que des comptes rendus (notamment ceux de J. Perrot, *Bulletin de la Société de Linguistique de Paris*, LIX, 2, 1964, 19–22; Alb. Maniet, *L'Antiquité Classique*, XXXIV, 1965, 288–291; et S. Ullmann, *Forum for Modern Language Studies*, I, 1965, 78–83) qui ont été consacrés aux *Grands Courants*.

Translator's Note

THE French original of this book, *Les grands courants de la linguistique moderne* (=*Travaux de la Faculté de Philosophie et Lettres de l'Université Libre de Bruxelles*, Vol. XXIV) was published in Brussels (Presses Universitaires de Bruxelles) and Paris (Presses Universitaires de France) in 1963.

The text of the English version differs in a few slight respects from that of the French edition. In particular, the author has made a few minor corrections and has added a number of bibliographical details (see his note above). The translator is responsible for some changes including the following: (i) a few minor corrections to the bibliography and references to later editions of some of the works quoted; (ii) the introduction of references to English translations of French or German works quoted, where these existed, and, except in certain special cases, the dropping of references to French translations of foreign works; (iii) a few slight additions or modifications to the text itself, that seemed called for in view of the fact that the original text was written with readers having a French cultural background in mind; (iv) various notes (indicated by square brackets: [ ]).

From Antiquity to the Nineteenth Century

GENERAL linguistics, in the sense in which the term is understood today, is a relatively new science. Its rise and expansion date only from the first half of the twentieth century; yet its origins are to be found in the fresh interest in the study of language that culminated last century in the creation of comparative grammar. Comparative grammar, which came into being at a time when a new scientific method was growing up in all fields of research, has, at least in such favourable cases as that of the Indo-European languages, achieved astonishingly sound results and has provided linguistics with its essential technical infrastructure. Not that there had previously been no linguistic awareness or that men's minds had not been exercised by the problem of the diversity of languages spoken in the world. On the contrary, many scholars had investigated problems of language but usually with some particular outlook in view that did not provide them with an overall picture. Nevertheless, the research carried out by these precursors had gradually matured and proved to be of great value in showing the way to those who followed them, for the early comparatists, however revolutionary their teaching may have seemed, were in fact only the heirs, and sometimes the prisoners, of a past which we must now briefly survey.

The Indians. The ancient Indians first turned to the study of their language for religious reasons. The necessity of ensuring that no corruption or modification should creep into the sacred texts of the Veda when they were sung or recited during the sacrifices led to an effort to preserve them in their pristine purity. Later, the Indian grammarians—the most famous being Pāṇini (fourth century B.C.)— commented on the value and use of words and, with admirable precision and attention to detail, drew up phonetic and grammatical descriptions of their language that are models of their kind. These

I

were long forgotten but were rediscovered by western scholarship at the end of the eighteenth century and, as we shall see, provided the starting point without which comparative grammar could not have been developed. But these Indian grammars were purely descriptive studies relating only to Sanskrit. Furthermore, as they had been compiled by men who, in typical Indian fashion, lacked any historical sense, they did no more than classify the facts without any attempt at explanation.

The Greeks. The Greeks have left us no description of their language equal to that given by the Indians. It may seem strange that, with their keen interest in history and their love of anecdote, they have left us scarcely any worth-while information on the languages of the peoples they came into contact with. Herodotus, who has handed down to us so many precious details about the numerous countries he visited, did not feel obliged to give us the slightest information on the languages spoken there; it is only by way of anecdote and, as it were, by accident that a Median word is quoted in Book I of his *Histories*, an Egyptian word in Book II and a Scythian word in Book IV. And yet many Greeks—mariners, settlers, soldiers—must have learned foreign languages, but the knowledge that interpreters passed on to one another has been lost: there survive only a few scraps set down without order or method by one or other scholiast or lexicographer. The fact is that in reality the Hellenes, imbued with their traditions and convinced, not without reason, of their intellectual superiority, despised these foreign tongues that they deigned to study only for practical reasons. The term 'barbarian'—an imitative word originally referring to the twittering of birds—that they applied indifferently to all foreign tongues because they were as unintelligible to them as the chirruping of the feathered kind, soon took on a pejorative value. The antithesis Hellenic/Barbarian became one of the constants of Greek thought and so allowed the striking similarities between Greek and some neighbouring tongues to go unnoticed, and Alexander the Great's army returned from the frontiers of India without bringing back the revelation of Sanskrit.

If the Greeks completely ignored 'barbarian' tongues, they studied their own language with close attention, but on the level of aesthetics (stylistic procedures) or of philosophy (the adequacy of language for rendering thought). This last point of view is of particular interest for us since modern linguistic thinking, both in the mistaken directions it has followed and in its more successful ones, largely originates in these speculations of the Ancients. The essential problems facing philosophers at pains to work out a theory of knowledge was to define the relationship between the idea and the word denoting it; the great topic of debate amongst the Sophists and the ancient philosophers—and one that remained a live issue until mediaeval scholasticism—was whether language was created by nature or by convention; φύσει ἢ θέσει; in other words, is there any necessary relationship between words and their meanings, between the *signifiant* and the *signifié*?[1] Plato, who undeniably inclined to the theory of the natural appropriateness of words, took up the problem, as many had done before him, in his *Cratylus*, in which he skilfully expounds the opposing theses, whilst refraining from coming to any definite conclusion one way or the other. The *Cratylus*, the interpretation of which has often appeared difficult, has been a stumbling block to moderns who have usually attached too much importance to the central section devoted to 'etymologies'; the important parts from the point of view of the history of linguistic thought however would seem to be the beginning and the conclusion of the dialogue where many of the fundamental theses of contemporary linguistics (the relationship between *signifiant* and *signifié*, the arbitrary nature of the sign, the social value of language) are adumbrated if not actually sketched out.

But with Aristotle's researches, linguistic thought was to turn in a new direction, that of the construction of grammar. Taking the view that the external world, τὰ πράγματα, which is offered to us by nature, φύσει, is known to us through the impressions it makes on our senses and declaring that words are the symbols, σύμβολα or σημεῖα, and not the exact images of the πράγματα, Aristotle, in the argument about the appropriateness of words, adopted the 'conventional' thesis, but his essential merit lies elsewhere, namely in having been the first to attempt a precise analysis of linguistic structure. General grammar is of course for him only a part or aspect of formal logic, but the care he takes to elaborate—as an application of the theory of propositions and judgments—a theory of the sentence, the way he distinguishes the parts of speech, the enumeration he proposed of grammatical categories, place Aristotle and the Aristotelians at the beginning of a long tradition: both their way of looking

[1] [For a discussion of the terms *signifiant* and *signifié*, v. inf., p. 52, n. 12.]

at the linguistic data and the vocabulary they devised for dealing with them dominated linguistic thinking until quite recently and still weigh heavily on the teaching and methodology of our studies.

The Alexandrians perfected the details of the grammatical theories and grouped them into a coherent corpus of doctrines. The Τέχνη γραμματική of Dionysius Thrax (second–first centuries B.C.) became for centuries the model to which constant reference was made. The fact that there are in language, as well as manifestations of regular structure, facts that contradict this regularity had indeed been noticed by the Ancients, but this observation was used doctrinally to contrast those who wished to construct a grammatical system on the basis of the analogies and those who, on the other hand, based themselves on the anomalies: the result was a series of fruitless quarrels between the proponents of the two views, the analogists professing an essentially normative doctrine whilst the anomalists appeared rather as *lettrés* anxious to respect usage.

The Latins. The Latins, who, in everything to do with intellectual activity, were intent on proving themselves good pupils of the Greeks, adopted the same attitude towards foreign languages (except of course Greek) and neither their grammarians nor their philosophers realized the interest an examination of neighbouring tongues could have for the study of their own language. Even the constant confrontation of Greek and Latin (cultured Roman society was for the most part bilingual) was barren, as the Latins strove to make the study of their language conform slavishly to the 'rules' formulated by the Greek theorists whose ideas they merely adopted and propagated. We must, however, in all fairness make an exception in the case of Varro, who made a considerable effort to define grammar both as a science and as an art and saw, far more clearly than the Greeks, the nature of oppositions of aspect in the system of the verb.

The Middle Ages. The conceptions of the Ancients continued to dominate studies on language. It might have been thought that contact between Christianity and peoples who spoke 'barbarous' tongues would have broadened the field of research, that the translation of the Bible into Gothic in the fourth century, into Armenian in the sixth, into Slavic in the ninth, would have raised the problem of relationships between languages. But this did not

happen, as the evangelizers considered the languages of the Gentiles as instruments of propaganda and not as objects of reflection and study. The grammatical framework drawn up by Dionysius Thrax remained intact (and was to remain so until the Renaissance and long afterwards) whilst scholasticism revived, in the study of grammar (which was one of the three branches of the *trivium*, the others being rhetoric and logic) the old controversy about the appropriateness of words in the form of the opposition between the realists (for whom words were only the reflection of ideas) and the nominalists (who believed that names had been given arbitrarily to things). It was then, too, that the *modistae* (so named from the title *De modis significandi* given to a number of treatises) considered that there existed one universal grammatical structure inherent in all languages and that, consequently, the rules of grammar, *qua* rules, were completely independent of the particular languages in which they were actually realized.

Yet, long before the end of the Middle Ages, one man was taking an original interest in problems of language and in that of the relationship between dialects, an exceptional man indeed who was both a scholar and a poet of genius and to whom Italy owes not only the unity of her language but also the fact that she embarked at an early date on impassioned but often useful and penetrating discussions of such concepts as dialects, literary language, the vulgar tongue (the famous 'Questione della lingua'). Well ahead of his time, Dante, in his *De vulgari eloquentia* that was probably written in 1303, considered that the '*si* language' (= Italian), the '*oc* language' (= Occitan [Provençal]) and the '*oïl* language' (= French) belonged to the same group, illustrating his argument with examples. He also distinguished with remarkable precision fourteen forms of Italian dialects. Romance linguists today can revere him as an illustrious predecessor. Yet, regarding the distribution of the other languages of Europe, he indulged in far less reliable theories inspired by the myth of the Tower of Babel and the ensuing dispersion. But Dante was an isolated figure, and the ideas he put forward in this respect found no answering echo.

From the Renaissance to the end of the eighteenth century. It was not until the sixteenth century that, in the intense intellectual ferment of the time, a more favourable climate for serious linguistic study was created. The religious fervour of the reformers brought about the

B

translation of the scriptures into numerous languages and, though Latin remained as a universal language, the contempt that had long been shown towards the 'vulgar' tongues weakened and disappeared before the blossoming of rich and vigorous national literatures. Theological controversies made a knowledge of Hebrew, a Semitic language differing in structure from European languages, indispensable, and this inevitably led to linguistic comparisons. Finally, travellers, merchants and diplomats brought back from their experiences abroad a certain amount of information about hitherto unknown tongues.

The wealth of material thus acquired provoked astonishment and awakened interest. The need was felt for classifying the facts and presenting them, conveniently gathered together, for the careful observation of the cultured reader or the amused curiosity of the dilettante. A simple way of setting out the ever-increasing number of specimens of languages was to group them geographically, in the order in which they appear to the observer. This method has the perhaps negative but nevertheless real advantage of sparing the reader any rash speculation as to the features that languages do or do not have in common or as to possible relationships to be deduced by comparing them one with another. This type of geographical classification was already being adopted in the sixteenth century in polyglot dictionaries and in collections of translations of the same text—usually the Lord's Prayer—in various languages.

The earliest polyglot dictionary (1502) is that of the Italian, Ambrosio Calepino. This enjoyed such success that it was several times revised and expanded, and Calepino's name came to be used as a common noun (French *calepin* 'note-book'). In 1538, the celebrated humanist and theologian, Guillaume Postel, who had travelled through Greece and the Middle East as an emissary of Francis I of France, and had studied the languages of the countries he visited, published a little book entitled *Linguarum duodecim characteribus differentium alphabetum*, using the Lord's Prayer procedure. But the first important collection of this kind was Conrad Gesner's *Mithridates*, published at Zürich in 1555. The title refers to Mithridates, king of Pontus (first century B.C.), who had won the admiration of his contemporaries for his accomplishments— uncommon in ancient times—as a polyglot: Aulus-Gellius (XVII, 17) tells us that Mithridates could converse easily and without an interpreter with his subjects in every one of the twenty-two linguistic

communities in his kingdom! And, so as not to belie his title, Gesner gave on a folding sheet at the end of the volume the text of twenty-two different versions of the Lord's Prayer.

The idea caught on. In 1592 Jérôme Megiser published a selection of specimens of forty languages, increasing this to fifty in the second edition (1593) and to some four hundred in his *Thesaurus Polyglottus* (1603) which even incorporated the dialects of the American continent, discovered only a century before. In later centuries, a number of works attempted to encompass what was known of all the languages of the globe, gathering together specimens of scripts, collating short texts, drawing up comparative glossaries. The crowning achievement of studies of this kind was the edition, begun by J. C. Adelung in 1806 and carried on after his death by J. S. Vater, of an imposing compilation, also entitled *Mithridates*, the four volumes of which listed, on a purely geographical basis, some five hundred languages.

However, as soon as research began in the sixteenth century, another methodological principle emerged that should have rationalized the study of the relationship between dialects, namely the principle of common origin that makes it possible to classify languages in families. However, these early attempts were unhappy ones: the scholars who were intent on classifying languages regardless of geography started not from an examination of the evidence but from an *a priori* idea, that of the pre-eminence of Hebrew. For religious reasons, they considered Hebrew, the language of the Old Testament, as the primitive tongue on the basis of which all others were to be explained. In this, they were following a Christian tradition that seems to go back to the speculations of Alexandrian Judaism. This opinion, backed by the authority of St. Jerome—it occurs, too, in Isidore of Seville—was to be taken up and maintained by a number of scholars including G. Postel who, at the same time as he published his *Alphabetum*, referred to above, also brought out a little volume with the suggestive enough title *De originibus seu de Hebraicae linguae et gentis antiquitate, deque variarum linguarum affinitate*. Such a conception clearly led to an impasse, for similarities between European languages and Hebrew, a Semitic dialect of a completely different type, can only be found by distorting the form and meaning of the words.

Joseph-Justus Scaliger had a sounder idea when, in his *Diatriba de Europaeorum linguis*, dealing only with the languages of Europe, he distinguished eleven languages that he considered as *matrices* from which the *propagines* had emerged (and were therefore inter-related). The four main 'stock languages' were indicated by their word for 'God': *Boge*, *Godt*, *Deus* and Θεός—i.e. precisely the Slavic, Germanic and Romance languages, and Greek. Errors of presentation and gaps there certainly were, but in general there was a lucid view of the problems involved, a good sense and prudence not customary at that period and the beginnings of correct method, the proposed parallels being justified by means of examples.

Unfortunately, for more than two centuries theorists, with their passion for systematization, generally speaking followed Postel. They clung against all the evidence to the theory of monogenesis, one particular dialect—usually Hebrew—being considered as the parent language from which all the others issued.

It is a curious fact that the patent lack of success of research, the precariousness of the results obtained, the impossibility of clearly defining the links between Hebrew—or any other dialect arbitrarily chosen as the 'primitive' one—and the languages alleged to be derived from it, in no way discouraged well-meaning spirits, so powerful were the urge to conform and, as far as the view that all languages derived from Hebrew was concerned, the anxiety to remain within the bounds of a certain interpretation, a mistaken one as it happens, of Holy Writ. In the early eighteenth century, Leibniz vigorously and rightly opposed the hypothesis of the Hebrew origin of languages, but his protest met with no response, any more than did his shrewd advice on the best way to study human languages: to examine the earliest written texts and compare them with the latest stages of modern languages. It is true that, as if he wanted to invalidate the very sound methodological principles he had just enunciated, he at the same time constructed on no serious foundations a genealogical system showing all the languages of Europe and Asia—and indeed of Africa and America—as deriving from a common prototype.

Another original investigator, whose work however remained isolated and almost unknown until recently, was the Italian, Giambattista Vico, whose *Scienza nuova* dates from 1725. In this work he proposes a *storia ideal eterna* conceived of as a cyclical history of mankind in three stages: theocratic (religious awe before natural phenomena leading to belief in a powerful being), heroic (an aristocratic society) and democratic (the rational stage in which justice and civilization flourish to the full); but, having thus arrived at its peak, mankind becomes corrupted and returns to barbarism, for its evolution is marked by repeated ebb and flow. Vico draws the inferences concerning language of this conception of history and the gnoseological principle that is at the basis of his theory of knowledge (the mind knows only what it does, therefore the social world, the causes of which are within us, is knowable by us; on the contrary, we can have only an awareness of natural phenomena, of which God is the author). The language of the first age was mute, men communicating with one another by means of signs; the first articulate language was symbolic, that is, poetic, and men expressed themselves quite naturally in verse;[2] finally the third stage of language is human language composed of words to which human societies can attach any meaning they choose. It follows that the interpretation of primitive legends and fables is of the utmost importance for our understanding of ancient societies just as the study of linguistic symbolism (figures of style, metaphors, vivid appellations) is essential for the history of languages. Languages too, like human societies, once they have reached their peak are affected by the process of decline, witness our Middle Ages in which poetry prevailed over prose and the 'vulgar', unwritten languages replaced the ordered beauty of literary Latin of the classical period.

This poetic vision of human language certainly represented a departure from the well-trodden paths of the past, just as the numerous works we have briefly mentioned that tried, more or less successfully, to classify the languages of the world were evidence of a new outlook. At least, people were becoming aware of the great number and infinite diversity of languages and the problems posed by this very diversity. On the other hand, reflections on the nature of language in the seventeenth and eighteenth centuries and attempts to analyse linguistic structure merely continue and prolong

[2] Vico was the first—apart from d'Aubignac whose *Conjectures*, 1715, he was unaware of—to suggest that the name of Homer in fact covered a number of rhapsodes whose activity spanned a period of several centuries. F.-A. Wolf, in his famous *Prolegomena ad Homerum*, 1795, does not refer to Vico, and it is unlikely that he was acquainted with his work which at the time was virtually unknown outside Italy. Unless we are mistaken, Victor Bérard does not seem to have mentioned Vico's opinion even in his polemical writings directed against Wolf; at any rate, the 'Homeric calendar' at the beginning of his *Résurrection d'Homère*, Paris, 1930, contains no mention of the author of the *Scienza nuova*.

the preoccupations of the Ancients. The continuing prestige of Aristotle is strikingly illustrated by the phenomenal success of the first edition (1660) of the *Grammaire générale et raisonnée* of Port-Royal, a work which, for over two hundred years and in the whole western world, was to serve as a handbook of grammar. The very title is indicative of the conception that Arnauld, as a good logician and keen disciple of Descartes, had of the study of language. Like his master, he proceeds from cause to effect, i.e. from reasoning to language. Sweeping aside the observations based on good sense that Vaugelas had expressed some years before in his famous *Remarques sur la langue française* (1637), the aim of which was to observe and describe—two hundred years were to elapse before there was a return to this sound method—the grammar of Port-Royal seeks to explain the facts, to demonstrate that language, as the reflection of thought, is founded on Reason, in short to construct according to logic a kind of schema of language into which the multifarious aspects of language as it really is must, willy nilly, be made to fit.

Through its successive editions and through the countless other grammars based on it, the *Grammaire générale* was to dominate grammatical studies for a long time to come. Even a man like Condillac, when (in the tradition of empirical philosophers) he ponders on the origin of language (which Arnauld had not done) and seeks to establish how languages have constituted themselves into systems, in order to analyse them reverts to the logical methods of Port-Royal. It was only in the nineteenth century that abstract reasoning of this kind generally lost face before the broadening of the horizons brought about by the knowledge of an ever-increasing number of languages, by a newly-awakened interest in living dialects, and above all by the development of an historical method which, rejecting all *a priori* considerations, starts from an awareness of things as they really are and works on observable facts. The reconstruction, on new foundations, of contemporary linguistic thinking was a consequence of the formation and development of comparative grammar. We must therefore begin our study of contemporary linguistics by examining the new conditions thus created.

PART ONE

The Formation of Linguistic Method

The precursors. It was the concept of the relationship of languages that set linguistics moving in a rational direction. The starting point was the discovery of Sanskrit by western scholars. Knowledge of Sanskrit (quite apart from the fact that, at least in certain instances, the word can easily be analysed into its constituent parts) opened the way to the corpus of work of the Indian grammarians, a treasure house of precise observations that were particularly instructive for the classification of phonemes and theories of the root and of word-formation. The West had been in contact with India since the sixteenth century, but the isolated observations a few shrewd minds had been able to make on the similarity between Sanskrit and the languages of Europe remained a dead letter. The Italian Sassetti, for example, who lived at Goa from 1583 to 1588, had noted in his *Lettere*, which were not published until 1855, correspondences between Sanskrit and Italian (such as *śáṣ/ sei, saptá/ sette, aṣṭaú/ otto, náva/ nove, devá/ dio, sarpá/ serpe*). The similarity between Sanskrit and the languages of Europe and a probable relationship between them were observed in 1767 by a French Jesuit stationed at Pondicherry, Cœurdoux, in a note to the Académie des Inscriptions, in which he set down his reflections on the 'curious analogies between the Sanskrit language and Latin and Greek' (such as Sk. *dána*: Lat. *dōnum*; Sk. *vidhávā*: Lat. *vidua*; Sk. *ásmi*: Gr. εἰμι). But this note, which was not published until forty years later, attracted no attention at the time.

The direction to be followed was shown in 1786 in a speech by a Bengal judge, Sir William Jones, to the Asiatic Society of Calcutta. He pointed out in precise terms the formal affinities between Latin, Greek and Sanskrit, affinities that proved that these languages had a common origin and that could not, he maintained, be explained if they derived one from another. He even supposed that Gothic and

Celtic had the same origin. He thus formulated two notions—that of linguistic relationships and that of a common prototype—that laid the foundations for a scientific study of linguistic families. Some years later the Austrian Carmelite Paulin de Saint Barthélémy brought in Germanic and wrote in 1802: 'quamvis enim Germani, Graeci, Latini et Indi maximis locorum interuallis inter se sint disiuncti, eorum tamen linguae unam harum gentium eamque communem originem satis indicant, et omnes in unam primaevam familiam referuntur'.[1]

Meanwhile in Paris, at the École Nationale des Langues Orientales Vivantes (founded in 1795), a small group of outstanding scholars were teaching the languages and literatures of the Near East. It was in this learned milieu that Friedrich Schlegel acquired the elements of his famous book, *Über die Sprache und Weisheit der Indier* (1808), in which the expression *vergleichende Grammatik* ('comparative grammar') first occurs: 'the decisive point that will explain everything [= the relationship between Sanskrit and these other languages] is the internal structure of these languages or the *vergleichende Grammatik* that will give us completely fresh information on the genealogy of language, just as comparative anatomy has shed light on natural history'.

Bopp and the early comparatists. It fell to Franz Bopp (born at Mainz in 1791) to gather together the unquestionable proofs that these languages were related and thereby to found the comparative grammar of the Indo-European languages. In Paris, where he lived from 1812 to 1816, he began the study of the Persian and Indian languages (and also of Arabic and Hebrew) before publishing in 1816 a memoir entitled *Über das Conjugationssystem der Sanskritsprache, in Vergleichung mit jenem der Griechischen, Lateinischen, Persischen und Germanischen Sprache*, in which, for the first time and with brilliant intuition, a coherent overall theory was formulated based on the parallels between Sanskrit and the languages of Europe. In fact, the Danish scholar, Rasmus Rask, had already worked along the same lines, but his study, *Researches into the origin of the Old Norse or Icelandic Language* (*Undersögelse om det gamle Nordiske eller Islandske Sprogs Oprindelse*), though completed in 1814 was not published until 1818, two years after the appearance of Bopp's work. The two

[1] Cf. Ludo Rocher, 'Paulinus a Sancto Bartholomaeo on the Kinship of the Languages of India and Europe', in *The Adyar Library Bulletin*, XXV, 1961, 321–352.

had worked independently and arrived at the same result: Rask showed, more conclusively than Bopp, the common origin of the Germanic languages, Greek, Latin, the Baltic languages and Slavic, but, unlike Bopp, he suffered from the disadvantage of not knowing Sanskrit; furthermore, his study, written as it was in Danish, could not have the same repercussion. Bopp, who was appointed professor at Berlin in 1821, continued his researches methodically and published his results in a series of five memoirs presented at the Berlin Academy between 1824 and 1831 under the general title *Vergleichende Zergliederung des Sanskrits und der mit ihm verwandten Sprachen*. Finally, in 1833, he began publishing a *Vergleichende Grammatik*, the first of its kind, which was not completed until 1849. Bopp's initial work compared Sanskrit, Greek, Latin, Persian and Germanic (Gothic and German); in the *Vergleichende Grammatik* he added Zend, Lithuanian and, from Vol. II onwards, Old Slavic; Armenian figured in the title of the second edition (1857).

Another who helped to further comparative grammar in its early days was Jacob Grimm who, introducing into linguistics the notion of historical perspective, devoted himself to the study of the Germanic dialects and, in the second edition of his *Deutsche Grammatik* (1822), published the results of his detailed research into the phonetic history of the Germanic languages. But the law named after him ('Grimm's Law') had already been indicated by Rask in 1818 and by J. H. Bredsdorff in 1821.[2] This was the *Lautverschiebung* (sound shift), an important discovery, for it was the model for all the sound laws (setting out the regularity with which sound changes occur in language) that are the basis of historical linguistics. Finally, it must be mentioned that F. Pott was the first to notice and state publicly that, unless precise rules are rigorously observed, etymology is no more than a capricious game. His *Etymologische Forschungen* (1833–36) laid down principles that might well still be brought to the attention of those amateur 'linguists' who conceive of an etymological 'science' accommodating enough to lend itself to all their fanciful meanderings.

Once the initial impetus had been given, the fever for resurrecting the past rapidly won more adepts to the new science. A brilliant band

---

[2] Holger Pedersen, *Linguistic Science in the Nineteenth Century*, Cambridge, Mass., 1931 (reissued under the title *The Discovery of Language*, Bloomington, Indiana, 1962), p. 260, n. 1.

of scholars eagerly set about the vast task of analysing the Indo-European languages and systematically studying them in all their aspects. New discoveries progressively enriched the stock of facts. Now that a clearer picture of the relationships between the different languages was possible, the earlier impression that Sanskrit represented, if not the original language (even Bopp had hesitated on this point), at least a stage very close to it, was dispelled. Each piece of evidence was closely scrutinized and careful attention was also paid to living dialects. A curious fact was the hostility of classical philology—then at its height—towards the new discipline. Classical philologists looked askance at these intruders who, with the aid of languages of which the classicists were ignorant and using methods they could not check, made pronouncements on questions of Greek and Latin grammar. It pained them to see these newcomers eagerly exploring a field they considered as exclusively their own. The philologists, with their passion for fine language and good literature, bristled at the idea that the study of the modern forms of Greek and Latin or of remote dialects like Sanskrit or Persian or, worse still, of uncouth Lithuanian or Scandinavian patois, could further their knowledge of Plato and Cicero. There is a well-known story of a Greek scholar who, when asked about a point of modern Greek, replied: 'Do you expect *me* to concern myself with a language in which ἀπό takes the accusative? Never!' The hostility was intensified by the fact that some comparatists, dazzled by the novelty of their research, were sometimes lacking in precision and built theories on facts they had not properly checked. And one sometimes feels that some philologists read the works of the linguists only in order to pick out mistakes in Greek accents or to criticize the barbarous turns of phrase that marred their Latin.[3] It was not until the end of the nineteenth century that philologists and linguists fully understood that they had a common interest in grasping one another's methods.

During this early period of the history of their science, the comparatists, carried away like the cultured society of their time by the consuming ardour of Romanticism, cherished for a while the fanciful hope of reconstructing by means of the comparative method, a 'primitive' state of language that appeared to them to be ideally

---

[3] Ludo Rocher, 'Les philologues classiques et les débuts de la grammaire comparée', in *Revue de l'Université de Bruxelles*, X, 1958, 251–286.

perfect. For, as Meillet said,[4] Bopp had founded comparative grammar rather as Columbus had discovered America: Columbus thought he had reached India, Bopp was hoping to recreate the original pre-Aryan language. Indeed, when in 1816 he published his famous memoir on the conjugational system, he made no secret of his aim: 'We must,' he wrote in his preface, 'get to know the conjugational system of Old Indian and make a thorough comparison of the conjugations of Greek, Latin, Germanic and Persian. In this way we shall see their identity and at the same time recognize the progressive and gradual destruction of the simple linguistic organism and observe the tendency to substitute for it mechanical groupings which have resulted in an apparently new organism when the elements of these groups have ceased to be recognized.' So, by comparing the Greek type δίδωμι, δίδωσι, δίδωτι and the Sanskrit type dádāmi, dádāsi, dádāti, he related the endings to the Greek pronouns μέ, σέ, τόν or, when trying to show that the endings containing *s* came from the root *es-* 'to be', he analysed (and here the influence of traditional grammar will be recognized) Latin amās 'thou lovest' as the equivalent of 'thou *art* loving'. It may well be that hypotheses of this type are not all implausible,[5] but they do appear to be undemonstrable, as they plunge back into linguistic prehistory. Bopp was attempting to arrive at a genetic explanation, being convinced that the attested Indo-European languages only represented highly evolved and therefore debased and deteriorated forms of the primitive language. The comparative method was supposed to make it possible to reconstruct the primitive stage of the language, the language of the golden age, a regular system which—every grammarian's dream!—had no exceptions. This idea that now seems childish or even pretentious was nevertheless at the origin of a host of remarkable studies and it haunted all the early researchers.

Schleicher. In the second generation of comparatists, one man proved to be an outstanding master and exercised a profound influence on the development of linguistics. This was August Schleicher who had first been trained as a botanist and throughout his life remained imbued with the methods of the natural sciences

---

[4] *Introduction à l'étude comparative des langues indo-européennes*, 7th ed., Paris, 1934, p. 458.
[5] Cf. André Vaillant, 'Hypothèses sur l'infixe nasal', in *Bulletin de la Société de Linguistique de Paris*, XLIII, 1946, 79–80.

and a devotee of Linnaean classifications. As an unrepentant plant-lover, he delighted in contrasting the linguist and the philologist, comparing the first to the naturalist whose study embraces the whole of the vegetable world, whilst the philologist is like a gardener who devotes time and trouble only to those species that have a practical use or aesthetic value.

The originality of his point of view was that he considered languages as natural organisms which, beyond the control of the human will, are born, grow and develop according to definite rules, then grow old and die, thus showing the series of phenomena denoted by the term 'life'. Thenceforward linguistics is envisaged as one of the natural sciences and Schleicher tried to define its laws with the rigorousness of the laws of physics and chemistry and to explain its evolution by applying to it the recently-published theories of Darwin. So, after the fanciful quest for the primitive language of mankind, a second myth now appeared in the history of linguistics, the myth of language conceived as a natural organism having an existence of its own independent of the individuals who use it. The growing prestige of the natural sciences gave added credence to this way of thinking and the topics of the birth, life and death of languages were thenceforth freely discussed: 'For a word, mark you, is a living being', as Victor Hugo put it in 1855.[6]

But Schleicher must be credited with having had a more rigorous method and a wider range of interest than Bopp (his senior by thirty years). In particular, his description of Lithuanian in his *Litauische Grammatik*, 1856 (such a careful study of a living language was at that time a novelty), is so complete and well-ordered that it is still found useful by specialists in the Baltic languages. His 'naturalist' conception of linguistics also had a salutary effect in that his followers abandoned the Romantic preoccupations of the pioneers of comparative grammar and strove to carry out their research with scrupulous care and accuracy and so prepared the way for the neogrammarians. However, in his studies in the Indo-European languages as a whole, Schleicher's interest in the natural sciences led him to oversystematize the facts. Out of a deep conviction that linguistic development was a long and inevitable decline (he once wrote: 'history is the enemy of language'!) he considered that the comparative method would provide information precise enough to enable him to

[6] *Contemplations*, I, viii, 1.

reconstruct the primitive state of language and (a paradoxical aberration when one thinks of the concern for strict method that characterizes the rest of his work) to realize the dream dear to the early comparatists: he had actually composed in 'common Indo-European' a fable entitled *avis akvasas ka* ('the sheep and the horses'). This naive and bold enterprise was doubtless the culmination of the touching efforts of linguistics in its early days to realize its impossible ideal.

Schleicher's name is also inseparably linked with two undertakings that enjoyed particular favour last century and whose conclusions are still widely accepted by the cultured public today. These were the attempt to determine in what way the Indo-European languages are related and to devise a method for classifying the languages of the world.

Schleicher set out his view of the break-up of Indo-European in the form of his famous genealogical tree. This *Stammbaumtheorie* implied that the one primitive language split into two languages, one of which in its turn divided into two branches, the Germanic and the Balto-Slavic (the ancestor of Baltic and Slavic) and of course the elements of each of these finally became the manifold ramifications of the languages that are historically attested, viz. the various Germanic, Baltic and Slavic dialects. The other branch, the Aryo-Greco-Italo-Celtic, was considered to have subdivided into Aryan (whence emerged Iranian and Indian) and Greco-Italo-Celtic, which gave on the one hand Italo-Celtic (the two branches of which in the historical period are Italic and Celtic) and on the other hand Greek. And so on and so forth.

In short, the method consisted in postulating the existence, between Common Indo-European and the attested languages, of a series of stages constituting intermediate linguistic units. It had undeniable pædagogical advantages, as the languages of the family could in this way be conveniently grouped in neatly bracketed and easily remembered tables—this perhaps is why the legend of the genealogy of languages has met with such widespread acceptance among the cultured public in general—but in fact it has the effect of setting up between the branches representing dialects or groups of dialects divisions that are much too sharp and do not correspond to the clear facts of history. Further, this type of classification was rendered possible only by stressing factors that seemed to support it and passing over those that seemed to go against it. This theory enjoyed great favour and was tacitly accepted by the neogrammarians, as is shown by the notions of 'Common Greek', 'Common Germanic', 'Balto-Slavic', 'Italo-Celtic', and so on, that they acknowledged and that are usually taught in the classic manuals of comparative grammar. Apart from J. Schmidt's reaction[7] against them, which had no immediate repercussions, these notions did not come under attack until the advent of Indo-European dialectology of which we shall say more later.[8]

The classification of the languages of the world—a division into three classes, isolating, agglutinative and inflecting[9]—was based on internal, i.e. specifically linguistic, criteria, namely on morphological structure. The first class is represented by Chinese, in which words are juxtaposed and grammatical relationships are expressed by the position of the words in the sentence, by their intonation and also by grammatical words having no meaning of their own, the words that Chinese grammarians call 'empty words' as opposed to the semantemes or 'full words'. In agglutinative languages, such as Turkish, grammatical relationships are expressed by agglutinating various elements on to the root, whilst in inflecting languages—such as the Indo-European languages—grammatical relationships are expressed by modifying the form itself of the word.

In fact, the idea of this tripartition goes back further than Schleicher to, apparently, the Indianist Wilhelm Schlegel, Mme de Staël's friend and brother of Friedrich Schlegel.[10] 'The languages that are spoken today or were formerly spoken by the different peoples of the world,' he wrote,[11] 'fall into three classes: languages with no grammatical structure, languages that employ affixes and languages having inflexions.' In any case, this theory, with some modification, is found in later works on linguistics or at least is present in some form in all speculations on the classification of languages. It was all the more readily accepted in that it provided a convenient framework for arranging the languages of the world somewhat after the

---

[7] Cf. pp. 39–40.   [8] Pp. 111–116.

[9] [Whilst the term *isolating* is universally accepted in English, there is no consensus regarding the other two terms. An examination of five well-known general works on linguistics reveals (i) that Sapir, Bloomfield and Robins use *agglutinative*, and Jespersen and Sturtevant use *agglutinating* (which is also given as the English equivalent of *agglutinant* in Marouzeau's *Lexique de la terminologie linguistique*), and (ii) that Bloomfield, Sturtevant and Robins say *inflecting*, Sapir *inflective*, Jespersen *flexional* and Marouzeau *(in)flexional*.]

[10] Cf. p. 12.

[11] *Observations sur la langue et la littérature provençales*, Paris, 1818, p. 14.

fashion of Linnaeus' botanical tables, the principle of which was at that time undisputed.

Schleicher not only adopted this approach but perfected the theory by using this tripartition to provide a general explanation of linguistic evolution. He had the idea of a cyclic progression of the three classes, proceeding from the isolating state via the agglutinative to the inflecting. In other words, before becoming inflecting, a language must have passed through an isolating period and an agglutinative period. Consequently, all known languages are at one or other of these stages according to the point of their evolution they have reached. Thus the tripartite classification shifted from the static plane for which it had first been invented to the dynamic plane and became the principle of a general theory of linguistic change. The development of languages was thought of as starting from a 'primitive' stage in which words are independent and are juxtaposed in speech and progressing towards an evolved stage in which, as relationships between words are now indicated by the improved method of inflexion, language appears as a more flexible instrument better fitted to express all shades of thought. This is a highly subjective position—one wonders on the basis of what principles it could be decided that one stage of language is more highly perfected than another—but echoes of it are still found amongst the 'progressive' linguists of the late nineteenth century.[12]

We must now refer to a paradox that will not have escaped the reader's notice. How could this same Schleicher who, as we have seen, was profoundly convinced that linguistic evolution was a long process of decline, have conceived of the idea of continual progress in the development of linguistic structure? As a good Hegelian, Schleicher is not afraid of reconciling opposites or at least of combining thesis and antithesis in a general theory forming a synthesis. Languages move from the first category to the second and thence to the third, which is the highest stage of linguistic structure known to us. But once a language, having undergone this constant process of change, has reached its most flourishing state and the richest and fullest stage of its development, it immediately begins to deteriorate, to lose this perfection that it had attained with such difficulty, and to enter on a period of 'regressive metamorphosis'. And as for the reason for this decline, it is, as Bréal ironically puts it, 'a fatality

[12] V. inf., pp. 43–44.

over the nature and causes of which Schleicher leaves a thick cloud hanging'. However this may be, Schleicher thinks that the life of languages falls into two parts: an ascending part that he calls the 'prehistoric period' and a descending part that he calls the 'historical period': a strange term when we remember that this so-called 'historical' period necessarily begins before we have any records since no language is attested at its perfect and ideal stage.[13]

Such a theory scarcely needs to be refuted. The idea of an evolution of structural types in the direction isolating > agglutinative > inflecting does not stand up to examination. Forms which seem to go back to a non-inflected stage of language may indeed occur in Indo-European and it was such facts as these that Schleicher and his followers stressed in support of their theory. But in comparison with these one could call on plenty of arguments to the contrary. The facts that we shall quote later from Chinese and English provide sufficient illustration in themselves.

The theory of tripartition, which was popularized last century by the brilliant writings of Max Müller[14] and given currency by most manuals of linguistics and little introductory works on the subject, enjoyed considerable favour because it was at least the easy way out. It provided a handy clew for anyone wishing to unravel the extraordinary tangle of the countless varieties of human speech. But we must reiterate here that linguistics is a science of man and not of nature and the human sciences cannot be made to fit into the rigid compartments and neatly bracketed tables that our colleagues in the exact sciences can draw up with enviable assurance.

In reality, the situation of the languages of the world is far more complex than the originators of this first attempt at classification ever imagined. A few examples will suffice to illustrate how unsound this theory was both as a principle of classification and as an explanation of linguistic evolution.

Chinese, an 'isolating' language in which as a general rule each word consists of only one syllable, distinguishes between these monosyllables by using a set of intonations varying in number from four to nine according to dialect (the extremes being represented by the dialects of Peking and Canton). The same monosyllable, i.e. the same sequence of sounds, can therefore have different values according to its intonation. It can be shown that this system of tones was

[13] *Die deutsche Sprache*, 2nd ed., Stuttgart, 1869, pp. 37, 47.
[14] Cf. p. 23.

originally closely linked to the initial syllable of the word, and in particular to a process of derivation by prefixation, a process that later disappeared. It is not impossible even that archaic Chinese may have had—as has been shown to be the case in Vietnamese—suffixes consisting of a single final consonant.[15] This is tantamount to saying that at an early period Chinese words were not invariable and that the language was then rather of the 'agglutinative' if not of the 'inflecting' type. In any case, the term 'isolating' is the less appropriate with reference to Chinese (it is all too easy to confuse the Chinese written word, which is inevitably an independent unit, with the phonetic word) since one of the most characteristic features of the language is in fact the way in which words are grouped together.

The Indo-European languages give the impression of being pre-eminently inflecting languages. Yet even in the ancient languages which have best preserved the flexional system there are traces of something totally different, such as those themes that function as words without having endings, e.g. the first term of compounds (Latin *arti*fex), the nominative and accusative of the inanimate gender (Latin *genus*), the vocative of the animate gender (Latin *lupe*), the imperative (Latin *fer*), etc. It is more than likely, moreover, that certain endings are elements that were once independent but became tacked on to the theme and finally fused with it. These are all indications of an 'agglutinative' or even 'isolating' stage of language, a stage at any rate in which inflexions were not much developed, or not at all.

In fact, it can easily be shown by careful study that no language corresponds strictly and exclusively to the principles underlying this notorious classification. French for example might be said to be an inflecting language since it contains vocalic alternations of the type je v*eu*x/nous v*ou*lons, but it is also an agglutinative language since it has a future tense of the type finir-*ai*, finir-*as*, finir-*ons*, etc., and also an isolating language with juxtaposed monosyllables the grammatical relationships between which are indicated by the position of the words, e.g. *Jean bat Paul*, which is not the same thing as *Paul bat Jean*.

In reality, a framework such as this tripartition into isolating, agglutinative and inflecting languages can only be drawn up if one

---

[15] On these problems, cf. for example H. Maspero, 'La langue chinoise', in *Conférences de l'Institut de Linguistique de l'Université de Paris*, I, 1934, 62–65; André G. Haudricourt, 'Comment reconstruire le chinois archaïque', in *Word*, X, 1954, 351–364.

C

stresses such features as are considered decisive and neglects those that go against the solution adopted. This means that certain *a priori* considerations easily slip into the exploitation of the norms of the system, especially when an ever-increasing number of languages has to be catalogued. One only has to stress one or other characteristic to obtain varying or paradoxical results.

English, in the course of its historical development, has almost entirely rejected two of the main characteristics of the Indo-European group to which it undeniably belongs, the inflexional system and the distinction between noun and verb. On the one hand, the forms of the verb are now almost invariable: in the present tense, only the 3rd person singular has an ending (*loves*) and in the past tense there is only one form (*loved*), the different persons of the verb being distinguished by the use of unstressed pronouns (*I, you, we*, etc.).[16] On the other hand, a word like *love* is both a noun and a verb and, by the process known as 'conversion', words that are really nouns can be used as verbs, e.g. *We tead* for 'we had tea'.[17] Because of features such as these, English closely resembles the so-called 'agglutinative' or 'isolating' languages,[18] so that it may reasonably be maintained that, structually, English is today closer to Chinese than to Latin or Greek or even than to another modern Germanic language such as German. An indirect proof of this is surely provided by the existence of pidgin English which has sometimes been said to be 'Chinese with English words'.[19] The English element does in fact predominate,[20] but that such a combination of English and Chinese has been possible at all is a direct result of the structural affinity (or apparent affinity, since there are differences in the way in which the structure is elaborated) of the two languages, in both of which 'grammar' in the traditional sense is reduced to a minimum.[21]

[16] The same is also true of the three persons of the singular in modern French: *je chante, tu chantes, il chante*, all pronounced [ʃɑ̃:t].

[17] Cf. in this respect D. W. Lee's interesting study, *Functional Change in Early English*, Menasha, 1948.

[18] People sometimes talk of the monosyllabism of English, but this is to confuse the written word and the phonetic word; English *you love* and *I don't know* really consist of only word each, just like Latin *amas* and *nescio*.

[19] J. Vendryes, *Le langage*, Paris, 1923, p. 347; English translation by P. Radin, *Language*, London and New York, 1925.

[20] Cf. R. A. Hall, 'Pidgin English and Linguistic Change', in *Lingua*, III, 1952, 138–146.

[21] A strange example is quoted in R. Gauthiot's *La fin de mot en indo-européen*, 1913, pp. 28–29, where it is noted that a feature of Bantu syntax (that is also widespread in Semitic), which consists in placing at the beginning of the sentence the noun to which

Briefly then, if the morphological classification isolating/aggluti-native/inflecting can sometimes be kept to a certain extent as one of the characteristics of certain families of languages (in which case it is merely superimposed on the genetic classification) it must be recognized that, apart from these precise cases, it has not attained the universal validity that a system proposing to catalogue all the languages in the world ought to have. Attempts have however been made to improve the method by invoking additional or more suitable characteristics. We shall return to this later.[22]

August Schleicher has to his credit a considerable output of work but few positive results. In spite of his admiration for the natural sciences and the amazing progress they were making by judicious use of the experimental method, Schleicher remained on the whole a man of the eighteenth century, intent on setting theory at the outset of research and making the facts fit into a predetermined logical scheme, whence the amazing *a priori* considerations that dominate his 'naturalist' conception of language and vitiate his work both on the reconstruction of Indo-European and on the classification of languages.

The same is true of his contemporary, Max Müller, whose works were also widely read. He had at least the merit of creating an interest in linguistic studies in Britain. But his ventures into 'comparative mythology' are discredited because of the rash hypotheses on which they are based and the oversimplified conclusions he drew from them, comparing the Indo-European myths one with another and considering them as lyrical paraphrases of astronomical and meteorological phenomena.[23]

The fact remains however that scholars like Schleicher and Max Müller had confidence in their discipline and succeeded in imparting to comparative grammar an impetus that, once certain errors of

attention is being drawn, and then recalling it by an infixed pronoun, is also found in spoken French; thus, the construction *ovandu meveisana* in the Herero dialect of Angola has an exact parallel in French *les hommes je les appelle* which is composed of two phonetic words that could be transcribed [lezɔm ʒlezapɛl], in which the first [lez-] corresponds to *ova-* whilst the infix [-lez-] is the exact equivalent of the infix *-ve-* of *meveisana* (the prefix [ʒ-] fulfils the same function as *me-*). Obviously, such considerations are typologically significant only if they occur in large numbers and especially if they fit in like manner into comparable systems.

[22] Pp. 120–132.

[23] It is only recently that a fresh comparative study of Indo-European mythology has been undertaken on a sound basis, by G. Dumézil; v. inf., pp. 97–98.

perspective had been cleared up, was to enable their followers to achieve constructive results.

The origin of language. As we have seen, the early comparatists hoped to reconstruct a 'primitive' state of language and so reach back to the origins of human speech. This illusion still persisted in the middle of the last century, and indeed even today some people have still not given up the idea of finding a solution to this insoluble problem.[24] This is a puzzle that has always stirred men's imaginations. Herodotus tells[25] how Psammetichus, king of Egypt (seventh century B.C.), wanted to find out which was the oldest nation of mankind, and so is said to have had two newly-born babies brought up by a shepherd and to have forbidden anyone to utter a single word in their presence. After two years the shepherd heard them say the word *bekos* which, on investigation, turned out to be the Phrygian word for 'bread' (the word in fact occurs in two Phrygian inscriptions), whence Psammetichus concluded that the Phrygians were an older race than the Egyptians. It is true that the children had been brought up with a flock of goats! There is also a story that that curious character, Frederick II of Germany (1194–1250) conducted a similar experiment which however was unsuccessful as the children died in infancy.[26] Three hundred years later James IV of Scotland is said to have met with greater success, as in this case the two children, brought up without hearing a single word of human speech, when they began to talk 'spak very guid Ebrew',[27] thereby confirming the commonly-held belief at the time in the pre-eminence of Hebrew!

Thanks to what had been learned from the comparative method, the problem was now to be tackled rather more seriously. Bopp's attempts to analyse the Indo-European forms into their primordial elements and Schleicher's theory of the primitivity of the isolating type had seemed to lay down more scientific foundations. So there was no lack of attempts to explain the origin of language. It was sought in the use of onomatopoeic forms, in the role of interjections, in the acoustic accompaniment of expressive gestures, what were

[24] V. inf. pp. 117–118 and p. 118, n. 180.
[25] II, 2.
[26] Ant. de Stefano, *La Cultura alla corte di Federico II Imperatore*, 2nd ed., Bologna, 1950, pp. 87–88.
[27] Cf. L. H. Gray, *Foundations of Language*, New York, 1939, p. 39.

the gestures and whose use was gradually perfected. It was also suggested that the origin of language might be found in auditory associations that could at first have been accidental and later became fixed. Some thought of a supernatural intervention or of a 'spontaneous appearance'. The language of animals was studied with a view to explaining how it may have become perfected and developed into human language.[28] It must be pointed out that observing the way a child acquires language sheds no light on the problem since the child does not create a language but merely imitates.

However interesting and indeed plausible some of the theories proposed, or at least some of the arguments advanced in support of them, may be, we have to recognize that they only amount, oddly called 'acoustic gestures', which later became independent of and can only amount, to a set of unverifiable conjectures. The linguist is here at a considerable disadvantage compared with the palaeontologist or the biologist. They have material going back millions of years to support any evolutionary theories they put forward. The fossil organisms found in the oldest strata provide comparative anatomy with invaluable elements for its reconstructions. The linguist however has to rely on written evidence alone for his knowledge of past periods. But the earliest documents go back at the most to the fourth millennium B.C. (the Sumerian inscriptions) and it is only for the last 2,500 years that we have any more numerous and more varied texts. These few millennia cover only a tiny fraction of the history of mankind and do not enable us to get back beyond a linguistic stage that is itself the result of a very lengthy evolution. Another way of explaining the origin of language that has all too often been tried is to make a comparison with the languages of primitive peoples. This is a tiresome illusion as the language of these so-called 'primitive' peoples is the result of a tradition that stretches as far back as our own. And there is also the question whether the mentality of these primitive races corresponds to that of primeval man.

The founders of the Société de Linguistique de Paris wisely laid down in the society's constitution in 1866 that the society would not

[28] A good historical survey of the various theories put forward is to be found in G. Révész, *Ursprung und Vorgeschichte der Sprache*, 1946 (English translation by J. Butler, *The Origins and Prehistory of Language*, 1956), Ch. III; cf. É. Buyssens, 'L'origine du langage articulé', in *Revue de l'Institut de Sociologie*, 1949, 377–406.

admit papers on the origin of language.[29] Their action was all the more praiseworthy in that there was at that time, as we have said, a prevailing optimism regarding the possibility of solving problems of this kind. Ernest Renan, who enjoyed widespread popularity, had indeed just written in the preface to the second edition of his essay *De l'origine du langage* (1858): 'If language is something created by human nature, if it shows regular progress and development, then it is possible by legitimate processes of induction to get back to its very origin'. The great Semiticist felt all the more justified in reissuing this essay (a first draft of which had appeared in 1848) in that the German linguist, Jacob Grimm, who was held in high esteem, had meanwhile (1852) expressed similar views in his book *Über den Ursprung der Sprache*. But Renan's programme now seems more and more illusory, at least in so far as one seeks to obtain results that are something more than unverifiable assertions.

Humboldt. Such were, during the first fifty years of research, the efforts that stemmed from an enthusiastic desire to lay (with varying degrees of success and sometimes with a mistaken approach) the technical foundations of a comparative study firmly based on facts. We must now turn back to examine how, from the time of Bopp's first publications, one man had attempted from the outset to raise the level of debate and to break away from studies of detail and construct a general theory of language.

Wilhelm von Humboldt, who exercised a far-reaching personal influence on German scholarship in the first half of the nineteenth century, had been profoundly interested by Bopp's work and by the horizons opened up by the discoveries of the young comparatist who was twenty-five years his junior. With his wide interests and his thirst for knowledge, Humboldt had clearly understood that language, which is a continuous creation, exists only as a manifestation of the human mind. It is, he said, an ἐνέργεια, not an ἔργον. Further, he considered that it is language that creates thought: just as numbers help us to calculate, so words help us to think. He believed too that the inner form of language (*innere Sprachform*) is a fundamental constituent of the human mind and that each form of language can therefore be considered as a characterization of the community that speaks it. Struck by the great differences of structure

---

[29] *Mémoires de la Société de Linguistique de Paris*, I, 1868, p. iii. This prudent clause was unfortunately dropped when the constitution was revised in 1878.

he found amongst so many diverse languages (for he had made a study of languages outside the Indo-European group, such as Chinese, Malay, Semitic, Basque and the Amerindian languages) he cherished the hope of establishing so close a relationship between the mentality and the language of a people that, given one, the other could thereby be deduced.[30]

Herein was the outline of a system of racial psychology the consequences of which Humboldt could scarcely have foreseen. This conception of a relationship between language and race shifted gradually from the realm of science (where Taine still placed it in his studies on the conditioning of works of literature) to that of a rather nebulous philosophy of history which it became when Gobineau gave it as one of the factors of his notorious 'inequality of races' and was eventually degraded to the role of a pseudo-scientific justification for the criminal racialist theories of Nazi Germany.

There is no need to repeat here the case against racialism or to reiterate that the factor of race has nothing whatsoever to do with linguistics. The somatic characteristics of individual human beings are irrelevant as far as speech is concerned. It is a proven fact that a child, whatever his race, has no difficulty in acquiring the language of his early environment. A Chinese or Negro child brought up in France in the same conditions as the natives of the country will speak French as easily and correctly as the French children he is brought up with. Ethnic characters are transmitted by heredity whereas the transmission of language is discontinuous. Every time a child learns to speak, the whole process of assimilating a language must begin afresh and the language an individual learns depends on the social group to which he belongs. History provides many examples of peoples changing their language as a result of wars, migration or invasion, without their ethnic characteristics being affected thereby.

If therefore no confusion between race and language can be tolerated, it is nonetheless true that a language may sometimes reflect the mentality of a nation,[31] but what we mean by 'nation' is,

---

[30] This idea was probably suggested to him by J. G. Herder's essay *Über den Ursprung der Sprache* ('On the Origin of Language'), 1772, which appears to have been the first systematic attempt to establish a relationship between language and ethnic type.

[31] We shall see later, pp. 103–104, the importance attached to this notion by linguists of the idealist school.

to put it more precisely, a social group, a body of individuals linked by common interests and traditions, by political and cultural ties. The factor of race does not, or does not necessarily, intervene in establishing national characteristics. One has only to think of the racial mixtures that the nations of Europe owe to the numerous migrations that have marked their history, or of the intermingling of peoples represented by the heterogeneous waves of settlers and emigrants who have helped to populate the Americas. Language is not necessarily one of the constituent elements of a nation. There are countries, such as Switzerland and Belgium, whose citizens do not all speak the same language. On the other hand, the members of some linguistic communities belong to quite distinct nations (e.g. the Spanish-speakers of America). What cannot be denied is that life in common within the same political unit creates a way of life, attitudes and reflexes that are typical of that community and constitute in effect, by opposition to other similar groups, what we call a national spirit.

Let us take one example. The French mentality and the German mentality present the observer with two easily distinguishable complexes of feelings, aspirations and temperaments. Can one go further and maintain, with Humboldt, that language reflects this difference in mentality? One often hears this said, and it is a commonplace to contrast French and German in this way: French is an 'analytical' language proceeding by a succession of clauses and clearly linked deductions, German on the other hand subordinates to one central idea all the incidental clauses, so that, as Georges Duhamel remarked, someone listening to a German sentence cannot understand it until it is complete, whereas a French sentence allows one to foresee the conclusion it is leading up to.[32] But is this not perhaps a *bona fide* illusion that confuses the characteristic way a mentality operates with the way it expresses itself? It is not to be wondered at that a language should reflect these admitted differences in mentality and indeed in what other way could we be aware of these differences? But to attribute to the language itself, to its structure, to its essence what it merely represents faithfully is to give psychology precedence over linguistics, which studies language for its own sake and not as a means for revealing the underlying mentality.

[32] Cf. A. Dauzat, *Tableau de la langue française*, Paris, 1939, p. 301.

One need only consider German as handled by a Frenchman or, conversely, French as handled by a German to realize that what is at issue is not primarily the language but above all the cast of mind of the person using it.[33] (The linguists of the sociological school were later to explain such facts as these by bringing in the social factor.)[34]

To be fair, we must remember that, after putting forward this theoretical statement on the relationship between the language and mentality of a people, Humboldt made no attempt thereafter to put it into practice. Indeed, he even declared himself to be sceptical about the possibilities of classifying satisfactorily the numerous and structurally very varied languages scattered over the surface of the globe. Later attempts to elaborate a psychological classification of languages on the basis of Humboldt's suggestions have not achieved any results that will stand up to examination.[35]

Humboldt was a strong personality whose teaching (most of his work was published posthumously) did a great deal for the development of comparative grammar, but in the most original part of his research—the study of the general conditions of language—he had no followers and the work in general linguistics that he had outlined was not to be taken up again until very much later. Likewise, the path opened up in 1867 by the work of an American of the succeeding generation, William Dwight Whitney, had no immediate repercussions. Whitney, who was opposed to any kind of mysticism, considered that language (whose function meets a need to communicate) was a human institution and that words were conventional signs. It may be thought that the reason why the work of Humboldt and Whitney had no repercussions is that their views were not understood, but the nineteenth-century linguists and particularly, as we shall see, the neogrammarians were concerned, and rightly so, with consolidating the foundations of their discipline and were preoccupied with perfecting precise methods of analysis, and so regarded with suspicion the general theories of men like

[33] Likewise Latin continued to be used by scientists of all nationalities until the nineteenth century. We are convinced that an attentive critic would in most cases be able to determine without much difficulty what was the mother tongue of someone using Latin in this way as a learned language.

[34] V. inf., pp. 93–97.

[35] Harold Basilius, 'Neo-Humboldtian Ethnolinguistics', in *Word*, VIII, 1952, 95–105.

Humboldt and Whitney, seeing in them metaphysical speculations lacking a firm basis rather than an attempt to reveal the mechanism of linguistic structure.

The neogrammarians. For half a century, linguistic research was uncoordinated and its aims ill-defined. An acceptable method still had to be found. But from the 1870s onwards, comparative grammar struck out in a new direction. The Romantic views of the purity of the 'primitive' language and the attempt to make a genetic analysis of grammatical forms were abandoned. It was recognized that the function of comparative grammar is not to assess known languages according to some ideal original system but to serve as a method for tracing the history, between two given dates, of languages belonging to the same family. After the various historical grammars which, on the lines of J. Grimm's *Deutsche Grammatik* (1819), had devoted more and more attention to living languages (F. Diez in 1836 and F. Miklosich in 1852 had begun publishing their comparative grammars of the Romance and Slavic languages respectively and J. K. Zeuss's *Grammatica Celtica*, 1853, laid the foundations of Celtic linguistics, etc.) so much precise work was being done on points of detail that similar attempts were made to eliminate all arbitrariness and to use as rigorous a method as possible on the level of reconstructing Indo-European also.

This was what a group of scholars, led by members of the university of Leipzig, tried to do. They were mockingly referred to by their opponents as *Junggrammatiker*, a title they were not slow to adopt with pride. In opposition to Schleicher's conception of language as a natural organism, they considered language to be the collective product of human groups. The positive method that they applied in all its rigour is illustrated by their proclamation of the existence of 'sound laws' and their belief that these operated blindly and of necessity ('Die Lautgesetze wirken blind, mit blinder Notwendigkeit,' wrote Osthoff.).

The works published at this time are perhaps somewhat laboured but they have nevertheless borne much fruit and are extremely valuable. Scholars were now scrutinizing the facts far more painstakingly than ever before, carefully tabulating the evolutions and correspondences that emerged and working out a solidly-based and coherent doctrine. A condensed version of all this research was given in K. Brugmann and B. Delbrück's *Grundriss der vergleichenden Grammatik der indogermanischen Sprachen*, 5 vols., 1886–1900.[36]

From the outset, then, the cause the neogrammarians championed was that of the proclamation of the existence of 'sound laws'. The prestige of these laws was enhanced by certain favourable circumstances. It will be remembered that the principle of the regularity of phonetic change had already been laid down by Grimm (after Rask) with reference to consonantal mutation. It had been observed that, corresponding to the voiced and voiceless stops of Indo-European, Germanic had voiceless stops and voiceless aspirates, and that these latter (which are unstable mixed phonemes) regularly gave spirants. So, the Gothic forms corresponding to Latin *dens*, *gena* and *tria*, *pecu* are *tunpus*, *kinnus* and *þrija*, *faihu*. For the second of these facts, one particular case seemed to confirm the regularity of the change: when the consonant was intervocalic, the Indo-European voiceless stop gave in Germanic not a voiceless spirant but a voiced stop: Latin *pater* corresponds to Gothic *fadar*. But the feeling of security induced by the observation of this fact was greatly weakened by the fact that there were exceptions to the 'rule', anomalies which also seemed to justify the lack of precision, the scorn for uniformity and the phonetic acrobatics that the early comparatists had over-indulged in, thereby bringing linguistics into disrepute. One had Latin *pater*/ Gothic *fadar* but Latin *frater*/ Gothic *broþar* in pairs that were apparently otherwise parallel, and, similarly, Latin *socrus*/ Old High German *swigur* but Latin *socer*/ OHG *swehur*. In 1877 the Danish linguist K. Verner[37] accounted for these apparent contradictions by noticing that the voiceless spirant remains when the preceding open syllable was tonic in Indo-European. Hence, the preservation of the þ of *broþar* is explained if we compare the word with Sanskrit *bhrátā* and Greek φράτηρ whereas the þ became voiced in *fadar*, cf. Sanskrit *pitá*, Greek πατήρ (and similarly Sanskrit

---

[36] A much revised second edition of vols. I and II appeared between 1897 and 1916.—[An English translation of the whole work by J. Wright, R. S. Conway and W. H. D. Rouse appeared under the title *Elements of the Comparative Grammar of the Indo-Germanic Languages*, 5 vols., 1888–1895.]—Brugmann published an abridged version under the title *Kurze vergleichende Grammatik der indogermanischen Sprachen*, Strasbourg, 1902–1904, which, under the general editorship of A. Meillet and R. Gauthiot, was translated into French by J. Bloch, A. Cuny and A. Ernout under the title *Abrégé de grammaire comparée des langues indo-européennes*, Paris, 1905.

[37] 'Eine Ausnahme der ersten lautverschiebung', in *Zeitschrift für vergleichende Sprachforschung*, XXIII, 1877, 97–130.

has *çváçuraḥ* corresponding to *swigur*). This demonstration was important since what had been thought to be a disturbing anomaly turned out to be an argument in support of the case for the regularity of the sound laws and their *Ausnahmslosigkeit*. Further, from the point of view of method, as Meillet rightly pointed out,[38] it established the absolute character of the principle that 'phonetic history is constructed on the basis not of similarities but of systems of correspondences; . . . the linguist operates not on more or less homologous concrete facts but on correspondences that may relate to heterogeneous facts'.

Saussure. Verner's article was in fact the first great triumph for the neogrammarians. The following year, a further advance came with the publication of a work that was to put the seal of success on the new school and bring about a renewal of comparative grammar. In 1878, Ferdinand de Saussure (then aged 21) of Geneva published his famous *Mémoire sur le système primitif des voyelles dans les langues indo-européennes*.

Of the five basic vowel timbres of Indo-European, *a, e, o, i* and *u*, Indo-Iranian retained only three. In this group of languages, the mid vowels *e* and *o* each opened to *a*, so that the three timbres *e, o* and *a* fell together as *a*. So, corresponding to the *e, o* and *a* of Greek ἕπεται, ὀκτώ and ἄγω and of Latin *sequitur*, *octó* and *agó*, Sanskrit has only *a*: *sácate*, *aṣṭá* and *ájāmi*. The role of Sanskrit in the formation of comparative grammar had given early workers the impression that it represented a state close to that of the original language and it was on the basis of Sanskrit and Greek (another language arbitrarily considered as archaic) that the sound-system of Indo-European was reconstructed. Schleicher for example, as a good Hegelian with a passion for tripartition, relied ingenuously sometimes on one and sometimes on the other depending on the possibilities they offered of forming triads: so, the vowel system was of the Sanskrit type (*a/i/u*) and the consonant system of the Greek type (π, β, φ, etc.). As long as the vowel system of Sanskrit was taken to represent faithfully the primitive system, it was also thought that Indo-European had only the vowels *a, i, u*, and so the vowels *e* and *o* of other languages were necessarily interpreted as having resulted from *a* in the course of the break-up of the primitive language. This was an arbitrary position that the *Mémoire* was to treat as it deserved.

[38] *Introduction* (cf. sup., p. 15, n. 4), pp. 470–471.

Indeed, as early as 1874, some scholars had, hesitantly and in piece-meal fashion, put forward suggestions implying that the distinction *e/o/a* could have appeared in Indo-European, but it was Saussure who demonstrated decisively the cogency of this assertion and the arbitrary nature of the converse hypothesis (the splitting of *a* into three timbres, *e*, *o* and *a*), and this long before experimental phonetics —which came into being only at the end of the century[39]—proved that such a process was physiologically impossible.

A number of problems were thereby cleared up at one go. The primordial role that the alternation *e/o/* zero plays in Indo-European morphology (Greek λείπω/ λέλοιπα/ ἔλιπον provides a classic illustration) was clearly demonstrated for the first time. Saussure also showed the workings of another typical piece of mechanism of the Indo-European languages, the delicately organized positive/negative alternation (*degré plein/ degré zéro*) of the sonants, and con-firmed the evolution *n̥* > *a* (that had been recently recognized by Brugmann), a surprising evolution in that a nasal consonant, *n*, developed into an oral vowel, *a* (neither, however, nor indeed their successors accounted for this process of which the present writer suggested an explanation some years ago).[40] In this way, the Greek alternations of the type τέν-ων / τόν-ος / τα-τός were satisfactorily explained. Going far beyond what was implied in the title of his *Mémoire*, Saussure built up a theory of the root which was to serve as a basis for all later studies. This was the pattern consonant + vowel + consonant (Type **ten-*) which, as a result of the flexible system of alternations of vowels and sonants, can take on extremely varied forms, so that some that had hitherto been thought aberrant now found a rational explanation. Finally, confronted with the apparently insoluble case of alternations which, in certain roots, seemed to fall outside the normal pattern *e/ o/* zero (such as the Latin type *feci/ factus*), Saussure imagined, for purely theoretical reasons, the existence in Indo-European of a phoneme (later called *shwa* and represented by ə) which had been an integral part of the very flexible system of sonants but had disappeared in the historically attested languages. Now, this solution, which appeared very daring at the time and was not easily accepted, was in reality a brilliant flash of insight as was proved by the decipherment, after Saussure's death,

[39] V. inf., p. 36.
[40] *L'Antiquité classique*, XVI, 1947, 321–322; cf. our *Stratificazioni* (v. sup., p. ix), 72–73.

of Hittite. In Hittite, which has taken our knowledge of Indo-European back to the second millennium B.C., the phonemes whose nature and function Saussure had brilliantly imagined are actually found to occur.

Meillet. The *Mémoire* had a decisive effect on the development of linguistic science, and it is no exaggeration to say that, from 1878 onwards, the task to which a brilliant group of linguists of all nationalities were to devote themselves was none other than the verification and development of the propositions set out in the *Mémoire*. The time of halting first steps was over. Comparative grammar now constituted itself into a rigorous discipline with precise methods of its own. Saussure was invited to Paris by Michel Bréal (who had implanted comparative grammar in France by translating Bopp's manual in 1865) and from 1881 to 1891 he taught at the École pratique des Hautes Études. His teaching gave the French school of linguistics its own character and conferred on it a prestige that it has maintained ever since thanks to such eminent representatives as Antoine Meillet (died 1936), a man of great perspicacity and an outstanding scholar who, for close on forty years, was looked up to with unfailing respect by colleagues and pupils alike. Meillet was the author of a series of books that are of great value both for the precise information they contain and for the way the author mastered the difficult art of presenting clearly an often confused mass of facts. Though more modest in scope than the *Grundriss*, his *Introduction à l'étude comparative des langues indo-européennes* is another classic in its field.

The role of the neogrammarians. The researches of the neogrammarians in which precise deductions went side by side with profound erudition were justly held to be one of the triumphs of the nineteenth-century positivist method, so much so that many sincerely thought that, amongst the historical sciences, linguistics was not far short of perfection, and they were persuaded that the future would do no more than perfect or touch up points of detail. Antoine Meillet himself wrote in 1903 in the historical survey appended to his *Introduction*: 'In one sense at least, we seem to have come to a point beyond which no further progress is possible',[41] a sentence that he

[41] P. 410.

retained in the following form in the last edition published in his lifetime: 'In one sense, we had reached a stage by 1900 beyond which no further progress was possible', even adding that the discovery of new languages had not modified our view of Indo-European: Hittite, he said, 'does not require us to make any changes in the essentials of the views expressed here; it sheds light on a number of facts, but it does not alter the general theory'.[42]

And yet, since the end of the nineteenth century, quite apart from the fact that our knowledge has been strikingly enriched, the very foundations of comparative grammar and the way it is envisaged have changed considerably. Not of course that Brugmann's *Grundriss* and Meillet's *Introduction* are no longer usable, far from it, but, although we still cannot do without the facts they amassed and the classifications they propose, we have nevertheless now to use these works with caution insofar as their theoretical interpretation of the evidence and the picture they give of common Indo-European are concerned.

It is in their scholarly works along comparative lines that the neo-grammarians are seen at their best. The great pains they took to ensure that their research was soundly based and to say nothing that could not be immediately and thoroughly checked meant that they often became engrossed in studies of points of detail so that their scholarship sometimes appears to be characterized by rigid conceptions and precise but arid exposition and one is tempted to wonder whether they ever considered the languages they so carefully studied as anything more than dusty museum-pieces that they pored over with the cold, calculated pleasure of scientifically conducted dissection. In fact, they scarcely ever bothered to deal with problems of general linguistics, but were content to refer to Hermann Paul who, in his famous *Prinzipien der Sprachgeschichte*, 1880, had made himself the theorist of the school. Yet, in spite of the wealth of its contents, this somewhat involved and not always very clearly written book has not had any very great influence outside the German-speaking countries. And indeed in general the *Junggrammatiker*, with their over-exclusive fidelity to mechanistic conceptions and excessive attention to detail, failed to see the interest of the whole, or at least they deliberately refused to move in what they judged to be the insufficiently prepared and therefore risky direction leading to the construction of a general theory of language.

[42] 7th ed., 1934, pp. 479–480.

The intention of these remarks is in no wise to denigrate the neogrammarians or to decry their merits, which would be profoundly unjust for, on the whole, in the state of knowledge at the time, their work constituted a fruitful effort and prepared the way for future developments. We owe them an enormous debt of gratitude.

Towards the end of the nineteenth century there appeared the first stirrings of a movement the importance of which was at first unsuspected but which was to lead to a complete transformation of comparative grammar and linguistics.

Phonetics. In his thesis, *Les modifications phonétiques du langage étudiées dans le patois d'une famille de Cellefrouin*, 1891, the Abbé P. Rousselot prepared the way for linguistic geography[43] when he published the results of a virtually unprecedented investigation he had made into a living *patois*, in the course of which he had in particular studied as precisely as possible the sounds used by speakers of the dialect. Thereafter he applied to the study of the sounds of language the experimental methods of physics and physiology and created for the purpose a technique for analysing and recording by instruments, thereby becoming the founder of modern phonetics which, on the historical and on the structural plane, seeks to draw rational conclusions from experimentation and casts aside the largely theoretical teaching that linguists had relied on thitherto. Amongst Rousselot's pupils, particular mention must be made of Maurice Grammont, a strictly orthodox neogrammarian whose thesis on consonantal dissimilation helped to strengthen the concept of the regularity of sound laws, and of Antoine Grégoire. Grégoire, who was the first to introduce the teaching of phonetics into Belgium, was the shrewd originator of the study of the language of children, from the baby's first halting attempts at speech up to the time when, about the end of the second or beginning of the third year, the child has acquired the elements of the linguistic structure of his mother tongue.[44]

[43] Cf. inf., pp. 40–41.
[44] Antoine Grégoire, *L'apprentissage du langage*. Tome I: *Les deux prèmieres années*, Paris-Liège, 1937; Tome II, *La troisième année et les années suivantes*, Paris-Liège, 1947 ('Bibliothèque de la Faculté de Philosophie et Lettres de l'Université de Liège', fasc. LXXIII and CVI).

Semantics. The term *sémantique* was first suggested in 1883 by Michel Bréal who justified the introduction of this neologism into scientific terminology on the following grounds: 'The study to which we invite the reader is of such a new kind that so far it has not even been given a name. Most linguists in fact have exercised their wits on the substance and form of words: the laws governing changes of meaning, the choice of new terms, the birth and death of words and expressions, have been completely ignored or given no more than a passing reference. As this study, like phonetics and morphology, deserves a name of its own, we shall call it Semantics (*la Sémantique*) (from the verb σημαίνειν), that is, the science of meanings.'

Though Bréal created the word *sémantique* in 1883, the discipline itself was not absolutely new. Without going into the numerous comments made—though haphazardly and unmethodically—by the Ancients on particular points of vocabulary, it must not be forgotten that from the beginning of the nineteenth century the only possible foundation for comparative grammar had been a searching study of the words common to the different Indo-European languages. But this study was undertaken largely for etymological purposes. If groupings of words were proposed, this was solely for reasons of form, i.e. because of the phonetic or morphological relationship between them. In Hermann Paul's famous *Prinzipien der Sprachgeschichte* a chapter of some thirty pages was devoted to semantic changes ('Wandel der Wortbedeutung') which were studied and classified according to the logical principles inherited from Aristotelian tradition and that came to have considerable success: the opposition between abstract and concrete, specialization, generalization, restriction, shift of meaning and other processes of rhetoric: metaphor, euphemism, litotes, etc. Indeed, we should not forget that if, after Bopp, the nineteenth-century linguists were revolutionaries and innovators of genius as far as the comparison of the Indo-European languages went, they nevertheless remained faithful adherents of traditional grammar of the Port-Royal type. So, from the psychological point of view, Paul's analyses related to concepts rather than to words.

Whilst retaining some of the terminological distinctions used by Paul (such as specialization, restriction, metaphor), Bréal had the original idea of starting from the words themselves and trying to account for semantic processes without reference to pre-established

D

patterns. His book, some pages of which consisted of a vigorous polemic against 'naturalistic' conceptions like Schleicher's, was sub-titled 'The Science of Meanings' (*Science des significations*). It met with very great success both amongst the cultured public and amongst philologists and teachers in general, but it had a mixed reception from specialists and linguists and even provoked various polemical outbursts. Whilst Schuchardt, always ready to be in the forefront of the fight, did not hesitate to proclaim the importance of semantics for etymology, most comparatists, such as Gaston Paris and Antoine Thomas, maintained an unswerving allegiance to the dogma of the infallibility of the sound laws and expressed their misgivings at a 'science' which they considered to be fundamentally capricious and unregulated.

And yet Bréal was a man of his time and his *Essai de sémantique* was in line with contemporary research, if only by virtue of the following two characteristics: he was concerned only with changes of meaning and so remained faithful to the neogrammarian view that only the historical study of language can be a scientific one; and furthermore the various tendencies that seem to account for semantic evolution are represented as *laws* (the very title of his 1883 article in which the word *sémantique* first occurs is 'The intellectual laws of language', '*Les lois intellectuelles du langage*'). So here too Bréal bows to the prestige of the *Lautgesetze* and to the neogrammarians' concern with constructing linguistics on the model of the 'exact' sciences. Yet he reacts very sensibly against an excessively doctri-naire approach when he states in his preface: 'To bring some order into this research I have classified the facts according to a certain number of *laws*. It will be seen later what I mean by *law*, a term that is not to be taken in any imperative sense. Nor are they laws admit-ting of no exceptions, blindly operating laws as the sound laws are, if some of our colleagues are to be believed.'

Furthermore, Bréal's semantic research led him to the conclusion that linguistic evolution does not proceed 'straight ahead, without fluctuation or detour'. This implies serious methodological con-sequences for the apparently solidly constructed edifice that the *Junggrammatiker* had erected by choosing—this problem of *choice* is, as we have said before, crucial for linguistics as for all the human sciences—the data that supported their case and minimizing those that told against it. The result of all this was that the 'inventor' of semantics was virtually considered by the partisans of the sound laws to lack precision and method. It is typical that the five parts (in ten volumes) of Brugmann and Delbrück's *Grundriss*, in spite of the example afforded by Paul's *Prinzipien*, gave no space at all to *Wort-bedeutung*. And although Meillet devoted a chapter of his famous *Introduction* to vocabulary, it was concerned solely with comparison with a view in particular to determining the type of civilization that had existed in the 'world of common Indo-European'.

Semantics was conceived by its creator as an aspect of historical linguistics, and this was how, basically, it was to be studied for over half a century.[45] We shall see later how it has been completely rejuvenated in recent years.[46]

The wave theory. In the second half of the nineteenth century the *Stammbaumtheorie* had gained widespread acceptance amongst linguists. It appeared so obvious that proof seemed unnecessary. It was however a follower of Schleicher's, Johannes Schmidt, who in 1872, in a slight but methodologically extremely important work,[47] disputed this oversimplified view of things. Following up ideas expressed shortly before, with reference to the Romance languages, by Hugo Schuchardt—whom Schmidt ought perhaps to have mentioned in his book—he suggested replacing the image of the genealogical tree by that of waves set up on the surface of water when a stone is thrown in. These waves then spread out in ever-widening concentric circles until they come up against the waves set up by other stones. We ought to envisage the spread of dialectal features as analogous to this. The areas covered by each feature are marked out by lines (isoglosses) which, far from coinciding,

---

[45] Meillet, who had made no mention of semantics in his *Introduction*, gave a lucid account of the ideas of the sociological school on semantics in his important memoir, 'Comment les mots changent de sens' (*Année sociologique*, IX, 1905–1906, 1–38 = *Linguistique historique et linguistique générale*, I, Paris, 1921, pp. 230–271); Vol. IV (1913) of K. Nyrop's *Grammaire historique de la langue française* is devoted to semantics. We must also mention the *Wörter und Sachen* movement (cf. inf., p. 41), Gilliéron and linguistic geography (cf. inf., pp. 40–41), Bartoli and *neolinguistica* (cf. inf., pp. 104–105) and Ernout and Meillet's *Dictionnaire étymologique de la langue latine* (1st ed., 1932; 4th ed., 1959) which marked a departure by introducing the history of words into etymological research.

[46] Pp. 133–140.

[47] J. Schmidt, *Die Verwandtschaftsverhältnisse der indogermanischen Sprachen*, Weimar, 1872.

intersect and produce an intricate network of dialectal traits, so that the once unified area of Indo-European has given way to a wider area covered with a tangled web of isoglosses. For the rigid schema proposed by Schleicher, which divided the languages derived from a common stock into independent branches, Schmidt substituted the concept of linguistic continuity in space, according to which the dialectal areas belonging to the same original linguistic domain diverge more and more the farther apart they are and as a result of political, religious and social conditions. This *Wellentheorie*, which was an attempt to show how things must have happened, certainly left many facts unexplained and gave no indication of the actual complexity of linguistic change, but later studies showed that there was a good deal of foundation for it. At any rate, it was a welcome reaction against the contemporary ascendancy of Schleicher's dogmatic views.

Linguistic geography. Rousselot's thesis on the dialect of Cellefrouin, Ascoli's researches in Italy and Schuchardt's in Germany and Austria were the prelude to the creation of linguistic geography, whose methods were to be given widespread currency, around 1900, by the works of the French-Swiss linguist, J. Gilliéron. This new science, which grew out of the monumental amount of close, patient research that was condensed into the *Atlas linguistique de la France*, and drew its strength from the study of living dialects (everincreasing attention was to be paid thenceforward to the notions of loan-words, substratum and, more recently, superstratum)[48] studies the geographical distribution of forms and words and their areas of extension and tries to plot dialectal boundaries. Although linguistic geography was at first hostile to the historical method, it does in fact make a great contribution, thanks to the wealth of forms it provides that enable intermediate stages to be reconstructed, to tracing the history of words by considering them not as separate entities but as elements of a whole. It has been said that it offers a veritable geology of language, reconstructing 'from their present outcrops the successive strata of words that are in large part hidden

---

[48] So, with reference to French, one could take into consideration a Celtic substratum (the inhabitants of Gaul at the time Latin was introduced having been Celtic-speaking) and a Germanic superstratum (the traces left by the Germanic invasions); and the words that at various times have come into French from neighbouring languages, such as English, German, Italian, etc., are loan-words (or adstrata).

below the surface'.[49] Abandoning the over-simplified concept of analogy, that was often the neogrammarians' last resort to explain apparent anomalies (Gilliéron spoke of the 'bankruptcy of phonetic etymology'), linguistic geography concentrates on considering the milieu in which the language is steeped. This concern for basing etymology on a close relationship between words and the things they represent—a kind of biological study of language—gave rise to the *Wörter und Sachen*[50] movement. Linguistic geography also revealed what a multiplicity of isoglosses there in fact are and the way they constantly intersect with one another. Finally, what was learnt about the distribution of dialects dealt a fatal blow to the neogrammarian doctrine of the infallibility of the sound laws.

'Centum' and 'satəm' languages. In spite of the theses defended by Schmidt, Schleicher's theory of the genealogical tree had received implicit ratification from the neogrammarians to the extent to which the concept of filiation was invoked for the classification of dialects, as was shown by the notions, which they accepted, of intermediate units such as 'common Greek', 'common Germanic', or even 'Balto-Slavic' or 'Italo-Celtic'. However, there was little insistence on the details of dialectal distribution and the only isogloss that figured in Brugmann's work was the famous distinction between *centum* and *satəm* languages, so called after the form taken by the name of the number 'a hundred' in Latin and Avestan respectively, these dialects having been chosen as representative types of the two groups. However, the phonetic phenomenon on which this bipartition was based is in reality only a perfectly ordinary fact of phonetic evolution, namely the tendency of velar plosives, especially in certain favourable circumstances (e.g. when they occur before a front vowel) to palatalize and consequently to become alveolar or

---

[49] A. Dauzat, *La géographie linguistique*, Paris, 1922, p. 30.—An excellent survey of the methods of linguistic geography and its developments is to be found in I. Iordan, *Introducere în studiul limbilor romanice*, Iaşi, 1932, translated and in part rewritten by J. Orr as *An Introduction to Romance Linguistics: its Schools and Scholars*, London, 1937; a second Rumanian edition, I. Iordan, *Lingvistica romanică: Evoluţie, curente, metode*, Bucharest, 1962, has been translated into German by W. Bahner under the title: *Einführung in die Geschichte und Methoden der romanischen Sprachwissenschaft*, Berlin, 1962.

[50] This is the title of a periodical founded by Meringer in 1909, but the idea had been in the air for a number of years, and there was even a polemical discussion in this connection between Schuchardt and Meringer; cf. Kukenheim, *Esquisse historique* (v. sup., p. vii), pp. 90–91.

palato-alveolar fricatives. This is the type of development that, in the Romance-speaking area, resulted in Italina *cervo*, French *cerf*, Spanish *ciervo*, etc., from Latin *ceruu(m)*.

This distribution had been admitted all the more easily by the *Junggrammatiker* in that it coincided with a geographical distinction, as the *centum* languages represented a western group (Celtic, Germanic, Italic and Greek) as opposed to the *satəm* languages which formed an eastern group (Baltic, Slavic, Albanian, Armenian and Indo-Iranian). But new facts came to broaden our knowledge of the ancient Indo-European languages and change the course of our studies, namely the discovery of Tokharian and Hittite.

At the beginning of the twentieth century, a French mission found in Chinese Turkestan, in the heart of the Asian continent, texts that are in part translations of Sanskrit religious works but which also contain documents (letters, merchants' accounts, caravan permits) which prove that the language was indeed in everyday use at the time (the second half of the first millennium of our era). This was Tokharian, the decipherment of which, thanks to the existence of bilingual texts, was not difficult.

Some years later, in 1906, German excavations at Boghaz-Köy, a little village to the east of Ankara, brought to light the archives of an empire whose history was thitherto completely unknown and even unsuspected. The language of the majority of these texts, which are extremely varied in content, was Hittite, the interpretation of which was begun in 1916 thanks to the intuition of the Czech scholar, Hrozný.

The repercussions of the discovery of these two languages were considerable. Before they were discovered, it was not known that, amongst the groups of Indo-Europeans who had set off in quest of new lands to conquer, some, in the second millennium B.C., had founded a powerful empire in Asia Minor, whilst others had thrust so far east and had created in Central Asia a civilization which was to be engulfed in the sands of Turfan and Kutcha.

Another consequence of this enriching of the Indo-European domain was to upset the commonly held view of the relationships amongst the languages of the family. It would have seemed natural that the newly-discovered Indo-European languages, Hittite and Tokharian, should fall within the group of eastern dialects. However, the decipherment of them revealed that, on the contrary, they were of the *centum* type and so showed affinities with the languages from which they were geographically the farthest removed. Here there was, at least on the face of it, a paradox that was to prove highly instructive and that was to be explained within the scope of a new branch of study, Indo-European dialectology.[51] So, contrary to Meillet's opinion quoted above,[52] these new witnesses completely changed perspectives that had been thought to be firmly established and made it possible to work out new theories on the structure of Indo-European.[53]

The concepts of progress and perfection. It is only fair to point out that, amongst the second generation of neogrammarians, more than one sought to raise the linguistic debate to the level of philosophical speculation. We have already mentioned, and shall do so again, Meillet's outstanding role in this respect. We must also pay homage to the Danish phonetician, Otto Jespersen, who, within the limited field of linguistic evolution, tried to make the notion of *progress* the supreme principle of explanation.[54] Having apparently been attracted by the evolutionist philosophy of Darwin and under the influence of Schleicher who considered language as a living organism, he campaigned against the opinion, firmly anchored in the minds of the early comparatists, that the ancient languages, by virtue of the wealth of their grammatical forms, represented a superior stage in comparison with which modern languages were but poor relations. Jespersen, who carefully avoided appealing to hypothetical or rash reconstructions and limited his study to the examination of known states of language, claimed that, in the history of languages, the sum of changes shows an excess of 'progressive' changes over 'regressive' changes and those that cannot be considered to be one or the other; in other words, gains outweighed losses. And he invoked the fact that as grammatical forms become simpler there is less of a burden on the memory, that they are generally shorter, which means that less muscular energy is required, that their formation and syntax present fewer irregularities, that greater clarity results from the establishment of a fixed word-order, and so on. All in all then, we have an ensemble of changes that makes modern languages more practical than the ancient languages and consequently better fitted to cope with all aspects of human civilization. It can be seen that

[51] V. inf., pp. 111–116.   [52] P. 35.   [53] V. inf., pp. 115–116.
[54] Otto Jespersen, *Progress in Language*, London, 1894.—Cf. J. Engels, 'Y a-t-il du progrès dans le langage?', in *Neophilologus*, XL, 1956, 242–249.

this was a new aspect of the everlasting quarrel of the ancients and the moderns. But in order to 'rehabilitate' modern languages—if indeed any such need was still felt at that time—was there any need to venture a value judgment in the name of principles that are highly debatable, depending as they do on a subjective interpretation of the facts? For it would be easy—and just as pointless—to look at them from the opposite point of view and show, for example, that the simplification of grammatical forms is an impoverishment, that if the forms are shorter then they are less clear, and so on.

The dynamic concept of progress as Jespersen used it has as its counterpart on the static plane the widespread conviction that it is possible to classify languages according to a certain ideal of *perfection*. This provides endless fuel for quarrels between neighbouring linguistic communities and is exploited without scruple by those bent on arousing sectional or nationalist feelings. It is a fact that the popular mentality is all too ready to indulge in criticism of its neighbours and their language and customs. We need only point out that loan words often take on a pejorative meaning: French *rosse* ('nag') is something quite different from the noble steed that this word (*Ross*) denotes in German; the French *hâbleur* is someone who speaks boastfully like a Spaniard (Spanish *hablar* 'to speak') but the Spanish *parlador* is a braggart like a Frenchman (French *parler* 'to speak') . . .; and many more examples could be quoted.

The same illusion exists regarding acoustic impression. The Frenchman is convinced that the German word *zwitschern* is difficult and outlandish, without realizing that words like *vin, bon, banc, un,* that seem so simple to him require difficult articulatory gynmastics of foreigners whose own language has no nasal vowels. In reality, this notion of easy or difficult, pleasant or unpleasant, depends above all on the articulatory and acoustic habits that one acquires in early life at the time when one is learning one's own language. Subsequently, the principle of least effort readily makes anything that is merely unaccustomed seem difficult. Likewise with morphology or syntax or vocabulary. It is a truism that whether we find a foreign language easy or difficult depends on whether it is closely related to our own linguistic system or far removed from it and consequently whether it demands slight or considerable effort on our part. But we turn such considerations into a value judgment, which is quite unjustified.

Nothing could be further from Homeric Greek with its great wealth of flexional forms than English where words are virtually invariable. Yet there is no justification for comparing them on the basis of an illusory criterion of perfection. It is a complete waste of time to speculate whether Homer (whatever the reality behind the name), if he lived in Britain today, could by using English create with the same charm and epic inspiration an *Iliad* and an *Odyssey*, or whether Shakespeare, had he lived two thousand years before in Greece, could, in Greek, have infused his work with the same dramatic power. In reality, any man who has something to say can find in any language adequate means of expressing his thought. Authors who blame the imperfections of their work on their language are only looking for a feeble excuse. Descartes understood this when he wrote: 'Those who reason most cogently and who best assimilate their thoughts so as to render them clear and intelligible are always the best able to argue their case, even if the only language they speak is Breton.'[55]

If there are no internal criteria that can enable us to decide that one language is superior to another, there are external factors that create willy-nilly a *hierarchy amongst languages*. For the fate of languages depends not on any inherent value but on the fortunes of the communities who speak them. It was owing to the prestige of the culture of Athens and the brilliance of its writers (rather than to its political role in the fifth century B.C.) that its speech predominated and became the basis of the common language of the Hellenistic world, the κοινή. For, amongst the Greek dialects, no purely linguistic factor predisposed Attic for this role. On the contrary, when the Ionic and the Lesbian of Asia Minor and the Doric of Sicily had already become polished languages of civilization, Attic, until it suddenly blossomed forth in the fifth century, remained the backward speech of a country district of continental Greece. Likewise, it was owing to the military and economic might of Rome and the political sense of its rulers and, above all, the prestige of the civilization it served that Latin, the humble speech of a tiny area of Italy, conquered the peninsula and then spread to the whole Roman empire, over much of which it established itself permanently, supplanting a number of local tongues. The intrinsic value of Latin counted for nothing in this phenomenal expansion. Similarly today

[55] *Discours de la Méthode*, First part (ed. Gilson, Paris, 1925), p. 7.

the languages of the colonizing nations play the part of superior languages with respect to the native languages. It will also be noted that considerable prestige accrues to a language from having the support of a great and militant religion: so, Islam and Christianity have spread Arabic and the languages of missionaries, French, English and Portuguese, in Africa. On the other hand, however, it sometimes happens that, in the sphere of religion, a language that is not in general use and that is understood only with difficulty or not at all by the common people enjoys great prestige. Languages such as Vedic, Avestan and Latin continued or still continue to serve as sacred languages, long after going out of everyday use. This is due to the psychological prestige that in matters of faith— and faith is a factor of prime importance in a society—attaches to unverifiable data.[56]

However this may be, the hierarchy of languages is a social, not a linguistic fact, for it is a product of reasons that have nothing to do with language itself. If we turn again to Descartes's observation quoted above, we can say that a philosopher could indeed compose a philosophical treatise in Breton, but his work would be neither read nor understood, for Breton-speakers, who are either peasants or fishermen, are not interested in philosophy, and philosophers, who do not know Breton because it is not a language of culture, would remain unaware of the treatise.[57]

This digression has led us to draw attention to the social side of language, of which the neogrammarians had shown themselves to be aware, and we shall discuss later how,[58] at the turn of the century, French linguists, following strictly the teaching of the neogrammarians, applied themselves to stressing the importance of this aspect of our discipline. The effort made by men like Meillet and Vendryes to broaden the horizon of linguists and make them aware of the overall problems had considerable repercussions. Yet an authority such as Meillet, who was by no means a narrow-minded specialist but was gifted with keen intelligence, a taste for ideas and a genius for clear, thought-provoking synthesis, remained so

[56] In this case, the technique of writing may have played an important part, as it made it possible to crystallize dogmas and legends and encourage the existence of priestly communities entrusted with safeguarding doctrine and having superior knowledge to the ignorant masses.—Cf. E. Dupréel, *Sociologie générale*, Paris, 1948, p. 242.

[57] Cf. J. Vendryes, *Le Langage*, 4th ed., Paris, 1950, p. 407.

[58] Pp. 93–97.

steeped in his strictly positivist training that in 1923 he could still write paradoxically (admittedly with polemical intentions):[59] 'Experience shows that one new fact carefully analysed does more for the progress of science than ten volumes of principles, even good ones'.

Meanwhile, however, there had been the impact of Saussure.

[59] He was reviewing a work of Bartoli's (v. inf., pp. 104–105), harshly and somewhat unjustly, in the *Bulletin de la Société de Linguistique de Paris*, XXIV, 1923, 83.

PART TWO

Ferdinand de Saussure

WE have seen how in 1878 Saussure's *Mémoire* had opened up new avenues to comparative grammar and had been one of the major sources of the remarkable development brought about by the neo-grammarians in this field. Forty years later, another of Saussure's works, published in very different circumstances, exercised a decisive influence on another aspect of our study, that of general linguistics.

After returning to Geneva in 1891, Saussure continued his teaching at his home university and, in the latter years of his career, devoted more and more attention in his lectures to expounding a general theory of language. Yet when he died in 1913, all he had published, apart from the *Mémoire*, was some articles on comparative grammar, but nothing at all on the problems that had occupied much of his thoughts and his university teaching. Two of his pupils, Ch. Bally and A. Sechehaye, with the aid of their own notes and of students' note-books (Saussure's own papers were of little help as he regularly destroyed his notes after delivering his lectures), undertook the dutiful and delicate task of recreating Saussure's work by publishing in 1916 a *Cours de linguistique générale*[1] which is a synthesis reconstructed on the basis of lectures given by Saussure, mainly in the course of three years' teaching. The geometrical elegance of this work, published in such unusual circumstances, exerted a great attraction and in the 'twenties (the First World War having prevented

[1] Lausanne and Paris, 337 pp. The *Cours* was republished in 1922 with a slightly different pagination (331 pp.) which remained unchanged in all succeeding editions (latest ed., 1965); our references are to this revised pagination. On the recently discovered documents and the critical edition that they will make possible, v. inf., p. 63.

[The *Cours* has been translated into English by W. Baskin, *A Course in General Linguistics*, New York, 1959; translations of passages from the *Cours* quoted in the present book, however, have been specially made and are not taken from Baskin's version, of which R. H. Robins has commented that 'those who read French should use the original text' (*General Linguistics: an Introductory Survey*, London, 1964, p. 32).]

it from becoming widely known for some years) it became the keystone of linguistic thinking and the prime source of inspiration (whether the views expressed in it were accepted or rejected) in the field of general linguistics. Such were the prestige and power of thought of this man of whom Meillet said that 'he saw scientific matters with the clear blue eyes of the poet and the visionary'.[2]

Language is an extremely complicated phenomenon. In order to dominate its complexity and to avoid confusion, Saussure boldly broke with the learned and painstaking research of the nineteenth-century comparatists, of the kind in which the neogrammarians excelled—and which is indeed an absolutely essential task, calling for much patience, and one in which he himself had distinguished himself—and tried to lay down general laws and to make out of so many works of remarkable precision but that lacked breadth an intelligently thought out and solidly constructed synthesis. The work of this open-minded and clear-thinking man is particularly remarkable for the breadth of the horizons it opened up to scholarship. And the best testimony to Saussure's genius is perhaps the fact that many of the ideas he expressed today seem truisms, common-sense observations requiring no demonstration. Indeed, others before him, from Antiquity onwards, had had an inkling of most of the definitions he gave, but whereas their ideas were latent and so to speak formless, Saussure's outstanding merit was to have given them precise expression in well-devised formulae that sometimes seem paradoxical or extreme (they bear the mark of a lecturing style) and, above all, to have integrated them into a coherent system. The greatest tribute one can pay to the originality and vigour of Saussure's thought is simply to note that, linguists have since devoted most of their energy to discussing his ideas, to approving, modifying or rejecting them.

If we are to review the main trends of modern linguistic thinking, it therefore seems indispensable to make a preliminary survey of the *Cours* and draw attention to its main conclusions, or at least to those basic principles that have become driving forces whose influence has been particularly fruitful.

The arbitrary nature of the sign. Linguistics, said Saussure, is in reality only a part of a wider and more general science that he

---

[2] *Les Nouvelles Littéraires*, 8 Nov., 1924.

proposed to call *semiology* (*sémiologie*), which would study 'the life of signs in the life of society'.[3] The first thing to be done, in the linguistic field, is therefore to analyse the sign. The sign, Saussure declares, is *arbitrary*, a common-sense observation doubtless but one that he stated forcefully as a principle. The idea of 'ox' is linked by no inner bond to the succession of sounds that, in French for example, acts as its *signifiant*: [bœf] (written *bœuf*). It could just as well be represented by any other succession of sounds, as is proved by differences between languages and indeed by the very existence of different languages: the *signifié* 'ox' has as its *signifiant*[4] [bœf] (*bœuf*) on one side of the Franco-German linguistic border and [ɔks] (*Ochs*) on the other.[5]

The word *arbitrary* does not imply that the *signifiant* depends on the speaker's own free choice but that 'it is unmotivated, i.e. arbitrary in relation to the *signifié*'.[6] Saussure at once brushes aside a possible objection: *onomatopoeic* words would seem to indicate that the choice of the sign is not always arbitrary,[7] but onomatopoeic words are never organic elements of a linguistic system, and besides they are few in number and the choice of them (cf. French *glou-glou* 'glug-glug', *tic-tac* 'tick-tock') is in any case to some extent arbitrary, for

---

[3] *Cours*, p. 33. It is important that this terminology should be retained, and it is quite wrong to include under the heading of linguistics, as is sometimes done, methods of communication not involving articulate language. On the relationship between semiology and linguistics, see G. Mounin, 'Les systèmes de communication non-linguistiques et leur place dans la vie du XXᵉ siècle', in *Bulletin de la Société de Linguistique de Paris*, LIV, 1959, 176–200.—É. Benveniste has suggested that a distinction should be made between animal *communication* and human *language*: *Diogène*, I, 1952, 1–8; the dividing line between them is what H. Bachelard has called 'the threshold of language' (cf. for example *Revue de synthèse*, VIII, 1934, 238), a movement towards the intelligible which is situated at a much higher level than that which can be reached by even the most highly evolved animals.

[4] [For the terms *signifié* and *signifiant*, v. inf., p. 52, n. 12.]

[5] *Cours*, p. 100.

[6] *Cours*, p. 101.—For further discussion of this passage, v. inf., pp. 85–87.

[7] There is here, though it is not explicitly stated, an allusion to what H. Schuchardt called 'elementary affinity': by this he means onomatopoeic words of expressive language, evoking cries and sounds of nature, the development of which is not explained by normal comparative methods. So, the word for 'cuckoo' in such Indo-European languages as Sanskrit, Old Slavic, Greek, Latin, and Irish is, respectively, *kokilaḥ*, *kukavica*, κόκκυξ, *cucŭlus* and *cuach*, forms that are similar but that prove nothing about the ways in which these various languages are related. We may note in passing that in French the Latin word has survived only with the meaning 'cuckold' (*cocu*) and that the name of the bird is a remodelled onomatopoeic form, *coucou*. Cf. *Hugo Schuchardt-Brevier: Ein Vademecum der allgemeinen Sprachwissenschaft*, edited by L. Spitzer, 2nd ed., Halle, 1928.

they are in reality 'only an approximate and half conventional imitation of certain sounds (cf. French *ouaoua* and German *wauwau* [and English *bow-wow*]). Furthermore, once they have been introduced into the language, they are more or less involved in the phonetic, morphological and other developments affecting other words (cf. French *pigeon*, from Vulgar Latin *pīpīonem*, which is itself derived from an onomatopoeic form); this is clear proof that they have lost something of their original character and taken on the character of linguistic signs in general, which are unmotivated'.[8]

However, Saussure toned down the absolute character of his statement on the arbitrary nature of the sign by admitting that in the mechanism of language there are cases in which 'the sign may be relatively motivated. So for example French *vingt* "twenty" is unmotivated, but *dix-neuf* "nineteen" less so since it evokes the terms of which it is composed and others that are associated with it, e.g. *dix* "ten", *neuf* "nine", *vingt-neuf* "twenty-nine", *dix-huit* "eighteen", *soixante-dix* "seventy", etc.'[9] Likewise, the suffix *-ier* of *poirier* 'pear-tree' beside *poire* 'pear' recalls *cerisier* 'cherry-tree' (*cerise* 'cherry'), *pommier* 'apple-tree' (*pomme* 'apple'), etc. This is a morphological and semantic motivation that occurs to varying extents in different linguistic systems: modern French, for example, appears particularly 'arbitrary' owing to various factors such as learned borrowings (cf. pairs such as *aveugle* 'blind'/*cécité* 'blindness', *eau* 'water' / *aqueux* 'watery') and the fact that it is poor in compound words (contrast French *continent*, *gant* 'glove' with German *Erdteil*, *Handschuh*, etc.).[10]

It should be noted that the use of the word *sign* (*signe*) has sometimes involved Saussure and his commentators[11] in a certain ambiguity. In reality, after some hesitations, Saussure decided to replace the term *concept* by *signifié* and *acoustic image* (*image acoustique*) by *signifiant*[12] (there is an echo here of the Stoic terms σημαινόμενον and

---

[8] *Cours*, p. 102.—It will be noted that onomatopoeic expressiveness is due in reality to *a posteriori* phonic motivation, as is proved by the case of homonyms; French *tinter* [tɛ̃te] 'to tinkle', seems to evoke the acoustic impression it refers to, whereas *teinter*, also pronounced [tɛ̃te], 'to tint', is completely arbitrary; cf. S. Ullmann, *Précis de sémantique française*, 2nd ed., Berne, 1959, p. 110.

[9] *Cours*, p. 181.

[10] Cf. Ullmann, *Précis de sémantique française*, pp. 115–120 and 124–131.

[11] V. inf., p. 86.

[12] [The terms *signifié* and *signifiant* have been variously translated into English as *signified* and *signifier* (e.g. W. Baskin, trans. of Saussure, *Course in General Linguistics*, 1959, pp. 65–70; E. H. Sturtevant, *An Introduction to Linguistic Science*, 1960 ed., p. 3), *significatum* and *significans* (e.g. Elisabeth Palmer, trans. of A. Martinet, *Elements of*

σημαῖνον)[13] and he reserved the term *sign* (*signe*) for the whole resulting from the association of a *signifiant* with a *signifié*. To quote Saussure's own formula, 'the linguistic sign is therefore a psychic entity with two aspects', i.e. it is composed of an acoustic image (the *signifiant*) and a concept (the *signifié*).[14] It was on the basis of this definition that Saussure declared that the linguistic sign is arbitrary, i.e. unmotivated. For on the one hand, the *signifiés* (concepts) form a datum that we perceive through our senses, and on the other hand the *signifiants* (phonic images) are imposed on us by the pressure of society within a given linguistic community and form a relational system. The word is *arbitrary* with respect to the *signifié* but not with respect to the system.

The linear character of the signifiant. The *signifiant*, being phonic by nature, exists only in time and, consequently, can be measured only in one dimension. The whole mechanism of language depends on this principle which is one of the factors allowing of the classification of linguistic segments. 'In contrast to visual *signifiants* (naval signals, etc.) which can offer simultaneous combinations in several dimensions, acoustic *signifiants* have only the dimension of time at their disposal: their elements appear in succession to one another; they form a chain. This character becomes clear immediately one represents them in writing and substitutes the spatial line of written signs for succession in time.'[15]

The duality langue/parole. One distinction of the highest importance that Saussure made and one that has proved particularly fruitful

---

General Linguistics, 1964, p. 24), *signified* and *significant* (e.g. L. H. Gray, *Foundations of Language*, 1939, p. 16), whilst M. A. Pei and F. Gaynor, *A Dictionary of Linguistics*, 1954, p. 197, define *significant* as 'The complex of sounds by which a speaker gives expression to the *signified*' and *signifier* as 'The spoken or written expression which calls up a specific *signified*'. However, the French terms are frequently retained in English (e.g. S. Ullmann, *The Principles of Semantics*, 1951, p. 31 *et passim*; R. H. Robins, *General Linguistics: an Introductory Survey*, 1964, p. 26 [*significant* here is a misprint for *signifiant*, cf. note relating to p. 26 on p. 41]) and, in the translator's experience, are widely if not generally used in *viva voce* discussion in English; they are therefore adopted in this translation.]

[13] Cf. R. H. Robins, *Ancient and Mediaeval Grammatical Theory in Europe*, London, 1951, p. 26.

[14] *Cours*, p. 99.

[15] *Cours*, p. 103.

E

was that between *langue* and *parole*:[16] *langue* is the whole system of signs serving as a means of communication amongst the members of a linguistic community, *parole* is the use each member of the community makes of *langue* in order to make himself understood; in other words, *langue* is 'a system in which all the terms are inter-dependent and the value of one derives solely from the simultaneous presence of the others',[17] whilst *parole* is the concrete individual act of the speakers who use the system in a given situation. We see therefore that *langue* which is 'a treasure stored up through the use of *parole* in those who belong to one and the same community, a grammatical system that is latently present in each brain, or more exactly in the brains of a whole set of individuals',[18] is conceived of both as a social institution and as a system of values.[19]

It is undeniable that this definition implies giving *langue* a certain pre-eminence over *parole*, which is considered as of secondary importance as compared to the *langue*. Saussure made his views on this quite clear: 'In separating *langue* from *parole* we at the same time separate (1) what is social from what is individual, and (2) what is essential from what is incidental and more or less accidental'.[20] And again: 'The study of language is therefore twofold: one part, the essential part, has as its object *langue*, which is social in its essence and independent of the individual: this study is exclusively psychic; the other, secondary, part has as its object the individual part of language, i.e. *parole*, including phonation: it is psycho-physical'.

[16] [There are no generally accepted English equivalents of *langue* and *parole* in these technical senses. The terms have been variously translated as *language* and *speaking* (e.g. W. Baskin, trans. of Saussure, *Course in General Linguistics*, 1959, pp. 17–20), *language* and *speech* (e.g. Elisabeth Palmer, trans. of A. Martinet, *Elements of General Linguistics*, 1964, p. 34; J. Orr, trans. of I. Iordan, *An Introduction to Romance Linguistics*, 1937, p. 41— but thereafter Orr uses the French terms), *tongue* and *speech* (e.g. Marouzeau, *Lexique de la terminologie linguistique*, 3rd ed., 1951, p. 132; M. A. Pei and F. Gaynor, *A Dictionary of Linguistics*, 1954, pp. 119 and 160; L. H. Gray, *Foundations of Language*, 1939, pp. 15–18— but Gray also uses the French terms, e.g. p. 18: 'While *langue* is static in itself, any historical survey shows it to be in a state of change. Such alteration is due to the action of *parole*'). However, in practice, the French terms are normally retained in English both in *viva voce* discussion and in print (e.g. examples quoted above and also S. Ullmann, *The Principles of Semantics*, 1951, p. 27 *et passim*; N. C. W. Spence, 'A Hardy Perennial: the Problem of *la langue* and *la parole*', in *Archivum Linguisticum*, IX, 1957, 1–27; N. Chomsky, *Current Issues in Linguistic Theory*, 1964, pp. 23 and 26) and are therefore adopted here.]

[17] *Cours*, p. 159.   [18] *Cours*, p. 30.

[19] On this duality the two terms of which are coterminous and imply no contradiction, cf. H. Frei, 'Langue, parole et différenciation', in *Journal de Psychologie*, 1952, 137–157.

[20] *Cours*, p. 30.

But Saussure recognized that 'these two objects are intimately bound up together and each presupposes the existence of the other: *langue* is necessary for *parole* to be intelligible and fully effective; but *parole* is necessary for the creation of *langue*'.[21] Furthermore, it is when he uses *langue* that the speaker comes to modify existing means of expression or introduce new ones. *Parole* appears therefore as the motivating force behind linguistic evolution, as the link between diachronic linguistics and static linguistics, which Saussure, as we shall see,[22] declared in another connection to be totally independent of one another. An inconsistency, doubtless, that stems from a certain doctrinal intransigence and also from the desire, that is quite understandable on the part of a pioneer such as Saussure was, to assert emphatically, and if necessary at the cost of causing offence, new and more or less revolutionary attitudes. Further, when Saussure asserts that *langue* and *parole* are 'two things absolutely distinct from one another',[23] he is making an assertion which, *if taken in isolation*, is too sweeping and must be tempered by such a statement as this: 'Language has an individual side and a social side, and one cannot conceive of one without the other', or as the following,[24] in which, after examining the relationships between *langue* and *parole* ('these two objects are intimately bound up together and each presupposes the existence of the other'), he concludes: 'so, *langue* and *parole* are interdependent: the former is both the instrument and the product of the latter'.[25]

So, *langue*, an abstract system that is a social phenomenon, and *parole*, a corpus of individual acts of speech, are inseparably linked. They appear, and this indeed was how Saussure understood it, as the two sides of the same entity.

The distinctive value of the elements of language. Another of Saussure's principles is summed up in the somewhat casual formula: 'In language, there are only differences'.[26] In other words, the value attaching to elements of language depends entirely on their opposition to other elements, on their being different from other elements. They are therefore characterized not by any positive quality of their own but by their oppositional quality and differential value. This is an essential position that is heavy with consequences, but it must be pointed out at once that, in spite of the absolute and somewhat

[21] *Cours*, p. 37.   [22] Pp. 56–58.   [23] *Cours*, p. 38.
[24] *Cours*, p. 24.   [25] *Cours*, p. 37.   [26] *Cours*, p. 166.

extreme way in which the statement is formulated, Saussure did not underestimate the role of similarities in language since he was careful to recognize that 'the linguistic mechanism runs entirely on identities and differences, the latter being merely the counterpart of the former'.[27]

The antinomy synchrony/diachrony. The nineteenth-century comparatists and in particular the neogrammarians represented an essentially historical school, so that, in contradistinction to the tradition of 'general grammar', what they understood by linguistic science was simply the study of the evolution and comparison of languages, and the description of the linguistic data had in their eyes merely a practical and pædagogical value. Saussure strenuously opposed this view by emphasizing that scientific methods are just as applicable to the descriptive as to the historical study of language, whence the distinction he makes between *synchrony* and *diachrony* and, consequently, the division of the science of language into two parts: *synchronic* (or *static* or *descriptive*) linguistics studies the make-up of the language, its sounds, words, grammar, rules, etc., at a given moment of time, whilst *diachronic* (or *evolutive* or *historical*) linguistics studies the transformations that language undergoes in the course of time. These two ways of looking at the linguistic data are symbolized in the *Cours* by a system of axes:

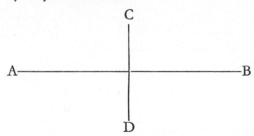

AB is the axis of simultaneity, CD that of successivity,[28] and Saussure not only denies the thitherto generally accepted primacy of the axis CD over the axis AB but goes so far as to declare: 'It is clear that the synchronic aspect takes precedence of the other, since as far as the speakers of the language in general are concerned this is the true and the only reality'.[29]

[27] *Cours*, p. 151.   [28] *Cours*, p. 115.   [29] *Cours*, p. 128.

And he goes further: not content with distinguishing between the two axes, he denies that there can be any direct relationship between them and holds that there must be no attempt whatsoever to study jointly temporal and systematic relationships: 'The opposition between the two points of view—the synchronic and the diachronic—is absolute and admits of no compromise'.[30] And as a proof of the absence of any relationship between the vertical axis and the horizontal axis, he adduces a whole series of examples of which the following is perhaps the best known. In Anglo-Saxon, *fōt* 'foot' has as its plural **fōti*. As a result of metaphony (*Umlaut*), a purely phonetic phenomenon having nothing to do with the formation of the plural, the *ō* of **fōti* becomes *ē* and then, as the result of a second sound change, the final –*i* falls so that the plural is now *fēt*, whilst the singular remains *fōt* (whence modern English *foot/feet*). We thus obtain the well-known pattern of the 'linguistic square':[31]

	fōt	fōti
Period A	fōt	fōti
Period B	fōt	fēt

Whereas in the vertical direction *ō* becomes *ē* by a process that has nothing to do with morphology and has brought about no morphological change, we can see that at the two synchronic moments of time, A and B, the formation of the plural (a fact of morphology) is effected by different mechanisms: in A by the addition of a vowel, in B by modifying the stem vowel, that is, in one case by suffixation and in the other by vocalic alternation. On the diachronic plane, therefore, *Umlaut* is a purely phonetic and purposeless phenomenon that affects only one of the two terms, whereas on the synchronic plane, in period B we have a chance situation 'which is seized on to mark the distinction between singular and plural';

---

[30] *Cours*, p. 119.
[31] The expression is not in the *Cours* but figures in Saussure's notes; see R. Godel, *Les sources manuscrites* (cf. inf., p. 63, n. 5), p. 47.

furthermore, it always relates to simultaneously existing terms.[32] Whence Saussure's conclusion: 'It would therefore be a fanciful undertaking to attempt to unite such disparate facts in the same discipline'.[33]

The object of linguistics. Finally we have the statement that concludes the *Cours*, and in a way sums it up: 'The one and only true object of linguistics is language envisaged in and for itself'.[34] At the end of this long meditation, the *Cours de linguistique générale*, what is defined as linguistics *par excellence* is what had previously been called internal linguistics as opposed to external linguistics. To bring out the difference, we may turn to Saussure's comparison with chess:

'The fact that chess was introduced from Persia into Europe is an external factor; everything concerning the system and the rules, on the other hand, is internal. If I replace wooden chessmen by ivory ones, this makes no difference whatsoever to the system, but if I reduce or increase the number of chessmen, this change has a far-reaching effect on the "grammar" of the game.'[35] The priority he accorded to the system led him to consider external phenomena as secondary. This way of explaining language solely in terms of internal factors was not completely new. Bopp and the early comparatists for example sought to study grammar for its own sake whilst the philologists considered it merely as a means of getting at the texts. But it is perfectly true that language had all too often been studied as if it were an integral part of other disciplines and investigated along lines appropriate to those disciplines. The philologist, the philosopher, the historian, the aesthetician, do indeed devote a good deal of attention to language, but they do not thereby engage in linguistics.

[32] Likewise, to say that the *a* of *capio* becomes *i* in *percipio* is to state the position wrongly. 'The truth is that *capio* can never have given the *i* of *percipio* but we are obliged to suppose that at one period we had *căpio* and *percăpio* . . .; then, at a later period, *capio* and *percipio* . . .; so, in the course of time, it was *percapio* and nothing else that gave *percipio*':

capio	percapio
capio	percipio

F. de Saussure, *Introduction du deuxième Cours* (cf. inf., p. 63, n. 5), p. 61.—H. Frei, extending this line of reasoning to the realm of meaning, spoke of 'semantic squares': *Cahiers Ferdinand de Saussure*, XVI, 1958–1959, 3–22.

[33] *Cours*, pp. 121–122.   [34] *Cours*, p. 317.   [35] *Cours*, p. 43.

We now know, thanks to the details that have recently come to light on the manuscript tradition of the *Cours*,[36] that the famous and often quoted concluding sentence of the *Cours* was not Saussure's own but an addition made by the editors. This discovery however in no way alters the programmatic role which, as we shall see,[37] it has played in the elaboration of linguistic doctrines during the last forty years.

[36] P. 181 of R. Godel's volume referred to below, p. 63, n. 5.
[37] Pp. 72 ff.

PART THREE

Linguistics in the Twentieth Century

THE *Cours de linguistique générale*, then, had considerable repercussions and its publication is sometimes considered, not without reason, as the birth certificate of modern linguistics for, amongst those linguists who have avoided being caught up in research on points of detail (which is indeed indispensable but can be too absorbing) and have tried to discover the general laws of language with the aid of a philosophical method, Ferdinand de Saussure was the most successful and his teaching bore the most fruit. And so, both on the plane of comparative grammar (see the 1878 *Mémoire*) and on that of general linguistics, we moved on with Saussure 'from empirical observation and the amassing of facts to the study of the inter-relationship of these facts within the system of the language'.[1]

Some of the views set out in the *Cours* have been the subject of long and fruitful discussions; others, considered as axioms, have given rise to a whole series of developments and extensions; and, as is to be expected, even the most fervent followers of the master, direct or indirect, have sometimes, whilst drawing the substance of their research from his teaching, moved off in somewhat divergent or even contradictory directions.

However, from the beginning of the century, linguistic doctrines were being worked out even before Saussure's ideas were given expression. As soon as these ideas became known, such theories were further developed either with reference to the *Cours* or, on the other hand, quite independently, or even in ignorance of it or in outright opposition to it.

On the one hand, then, there are the direct fruits of Saussure's teaching or at least the discussion of some of the key ideas of the *Cours* and on the other hand movements on which this influence

[1] G. Redard, 'Ferdinand de Saussure, pionnier de la linguistique', in *Journal de Genève*, 23–24 Nov. 1957.

has been nil or insignificant or belated. This suggests a framework within which we can survey the tendencies of modern linguistics. That there is a certain arbitrariness and a lack of respect for strict chronological order in such a way of going about it is not disputed, but could it be otherwise? In the human sciences, to which linguistics belongs, we are in the domain of the continuous, and rigid divisions into chapters and paragraphs have no more than a methodological value.

The Geneva school. In general, the supporters of this school have tried to remain whole-heartedly loyal to the teaching and spirit of Saussure. For a long time the two leaders were Ch. Bally and A. Sechehaye, who had assumed the responsibility of publishing the *Cours*. Bally, who tackled the difficult problem of the relationship between thought and its linguistic expression, renewed the study of stylistics by defining it as the study of the affective elements of language and by devoting his attention to the deviations that individual usage (*parole*) imposes on the system (*langue*). His work in this field,[2] work that he situated fairly and squarely in the synchronic dimension (only present associations are of value in stylistics and etymology must be discounted) is remarkable both for the strict logic that determines the plan of it and for the care with which he seeks to grasp the slightest shades of the procedures employed. Sechehaye applied himself to constructing a grammatical method (the psychological analysis of thought) that would introduce Saussurian conceptions effectively into the field of teaching. Henri Frei, who at present occupies Saussure's chair, has shown how instructive for the linguist 'mistakes' of grammar can be (mistakes committed by the speaker who responds in this way to the 'needs' both of communication—assimilation and differentiation, brevity and invariability—and of expression) and has made himself the promoter of 'functional' linguistics which 'seeks to explain the facts by considering them in relation to the functions (needs, instincts, etc.) that they are supposed to satisfy'.[3]

[2] *Précis de stylistique*, Geneva, 1905; *Traité de stylistique française*, Heidelberg, 1904, 3rd ed., Geneva-Paris, 1951; there is also his *Linguistique générale et linguistique française*, Berne, 1932, 3rd ed., 1950, which resumes the ideas he had stated in this field in the course of his career.

[3] H. Frei, *La grammaire des fautes*, Geneva, 1929.

A characteristic common to the linguists of this school is their constant preoccupation with classifying and interpreting the principles of the *Cours*, which, however, they insist that they do not consider as dogmas accepted without discussion. The recent discovery of some of Saussure's manuscript notes[4] and also of students' note-books that were not used by those who published the *Cours* has enabled R. Godel to publish an important work on the 'manuscript tradition' of the *Cours* that must henceforward be used together with the 1916 text of the *Cours* itself[5] and which is a prelude to the critical edition of the *Cours* that R. Engler intends to bring out.[6]

We shall have occasion to return later to the activity of our colleagues in Geneva.[7] Let it be said however that if the veneration with which they rightly surround the founder of their school has inspired many valuable publications, the jealous care with which they defend his memory against criticisms that seem to them to be unjustified has sometimes led them, in interpreting the text, into a certain intransigence[8]—it is perhaps not inappropriate in this context to quote d'Arbois de Jubainville's remark:[9] 'You call yourself my pupil and yet you've never contradicted me?'—and, in their conviction that the *Cours* represents the 'authentic' thought of Saussure,[10] into a touchiness that the recently discovered documents show to be sometimes excessive.[11]

---

[4] 'Notes inédites de F. de Saussure', published by R. Godel in *Cahiers Ferdinand de Saussure*, XII, 1954, 49–71; 'Souvenirs de F. de Saussure concernant sa jeunesse et ses études ', ibid., XVII, 1960, 12–25.

[5] Robert Godel, *Les sources manuscrites du Cours de linguistique générale de F. de Saussure*, Geneva-Paris, 1957; and the following articles published in the *Cahiers Ferdinand de Saussure*: (i) 'Introduction du deuxième Cours de linguistique générale (1908–1909)', XV, 1957, 3–103; (ii) ' Les cahiers E. Constantin', XVI, 1958–1959, 23–32; (iii) 'Inventaire des manuscrits de F. de Saussure remis à la Bibliothèque Publique et Universitaire de Genève', XVII, 1960, 5–11.

[6] Rudolf Engler, '*CLG* und *SM*: eine kritische Ausgabe des *Cours de linguistique générale*', in *Kratylos*, IV, 1959, 119–132; 'Théorie et critique d'un principe saussurien: l'arbitraire du signe' in *Cahiers F. de Saussure*, XIX, 1962, 37–60; 'Compléments à l'arbitraire', ibid., XXI, 1964, 25–32.

[7] Pp. 83, 87, 90, 132 and 136.

[8] See for example the polemical discussion between H. Frei and É. Buyssens regarding Saussure's contention that 'in language there are only differences', in *Cahiers Ferdinand de Saussure*, VIII, 1949, 37–60; IX, 1950, 7–28; X, 1952, 47–50.

[9] Quoted by J. Vendryes, *Cahiers Ferdinand de Saussure*, VI, 1946–1947, p. 48.

[10] See for example H. Frei in *Cahiers Ferdinand de Saussure*, IX, 1950, 27–28.

[11] V. sup., p. 59 et inf., pp. 86–87.

Phonology. Phonetics, which was formerly a science of observation—the ancient Indians achieved astonishing results in this field—and which studies the sounds of human speech from the articulatory and acoustic points of view, has been much improved since experimental methods were first applied to it at the end of the last century.[12] From 1926 onwards a group of linguists from the Linguistic Circle of Prague, arguing from the fact that phonetics, since it started using apparatus and to be studied in laboratories, has made enormous progress but at the same time has moved further and further away from linguistics, devised a completely different method for studying the sounds of language. At the first International Congress of Linguists at the Hague in 1928, R. Jakobson, S. Karcevskij and N. S. Trubetzkoy presented their famous *Proposition 22* which marks the birth of the new discipline of *phonology*.[13] The proposition dealt with the 'significant differences' that characterize the elements of every phonological system and of the 'phonological correlations' that are constituted by series of binary oppositions.

[12] V. sup., p. 36.
[13] The terms *phonétique* [Ger. *Phonetik*] and *phonologie* [Ger. *Phonologie*] that were used concurrently last century with reference to the study of the sounds of language had been applied by the neogrammarians to different aspects, *phonétique* to the descriptive and *phonologie* to the historical study of sounds. Saussure on the contrary applied the term *phonologie* to the physiological study of sounds (and was followed in this respect by Grammont in his *Traité de phonétique*) and the term *phonétique* to the study of the evolution of sounds; the French term *phonologie* is now used only in the strict sense given to it, at Jakobson's suggestion, by the Prague school.

[There is no unanimity amongst linguists writing in English on the translation of French and German *phonologie* in this sense. Traditionally, *phonology* has been—and indeed still is—widely used in English in the neogrammarian sense of 'historical phonetics', and for this reason many linguists avoid it in the Trubetzkoyan sense, preferring to use the term *phonemics*, which was indeed suggested by Trubetzkoy himself as the English equivalent of *Phonologie* in this sense (*Grundzüge*, p. 12—the text of p. 12 twice has *phonetics*, but this is corrected to *phonemics* in the errata, p. 298; French trans., pp. 9–10); *phonematics* has also occasionally been used. However, *phonology* is nowadays extensively employed—perhaps even more so than *phonemics*—in the Trubetzkoyan sense; it appears to be preferred by British linguists (see for example R. H. Robins, *General Linguistics: an Introductory Survey*, 1964, pp. 18 etc.; M. A. K. Halliday, Angus McIntosh and Peter Strevens, *The Linguistic Sciences and Language Teaching*, 1964, pp. 63–64, etc.) as well as by some American linguists, and for that reason is adopted here. For examples of the use of *phonemics* and *phonology* by American linguists, see E. P. Hamp, *A Glossary of American Technical Linguistic Usage, 1925–1950*, Utrecht-Antwerp, 1957, pp. 45–46.

It must further be pointed out that some linguists divide phonology into the two branches of *phonematics* and *prosody* (see for example A. Martinet, *A Functional View of Language*, 1962, p. 30).]

Starting from the principle that any science, to be valid, must be general, the members of this school wished to reintegrate phonetics into the framework of linguistics by rescuing it from the examination of the purely individual facts of *parole* and applying it to the more general study of *langue*. So, whereas phonetics is the study of the sounds of *parole*, phonology is seen as the study of the sounds of *langue*,[14] with particular emphasis on the relationship between the sound (or the complex of sounds) and its meaning. One might also say that phonetics studies what is actually pronounced, something that varies from one individual to another and even within the usage of one individual, whilst phonology studies what one is conscious of pronouncing or of hearing pronounced, and this is a constant within a given linguistic community.

The Polish linguist, Baudouin de Courtenay, was probably the first to put forward, last century, 'the idea that there must be two distinct types of descriptive phonetics, depending on whether one wishes to study concrete sounds as physical phenomena or as phonic signals used for purposes of mutual comprehension within a linguistic community'.[15] This was undoubtedly a promising idea but it had no repercussions outside a narrow circle and the promoters of phonology based their theories much more on the teaching of Saussure. The duality *langue/parole* had prepared the ground—indeed Trubetzkoy refers to it on the very first page of his *Grundzüge*—and, even more so, the affirmation that 'in language there are only differences': the whole of phonology, the basic principle of which is the differential quality, is there in embryo.

In Trubetzkoy's words, we can say that phonetics is 'the science of the material aspects of the sounds of human language' whereas phonology only envisages 'as far as sound is concerned that which

[14] The proportion $\dfrac{phonologie}{phonétique} = \dfrac{langue}{parole}$ derives

from Trubetzkoy (*Grundzüge*, p. 7; French trans., p. 3). It has been pointed out that the distinction is not as simple as this. There are, in fact, non-pertinent variants which are imposed and so are a fact of *langue* (e.g. the fact that, in French, final vowels are normally short is 'arbitrary' and is therefore a fact of *langue*, even though it would not be phonologically distinctive if one were to pronounce them long): cf. H. Frei, 'Langue, parole et différenciation', in *Journal de psychologie*, 1952, 140–141; André Martinet, *Économie des changements phonétiques* (cf. inf., p. 71 and n. 29), p. 18 and n. 2.

[15] N. S. Trubetzkoy, *Grundzüge der Phonologie*, Prague, 1939, 2nd ed., Göttingen, 1958 (our references are to the 2nd ed.), p. 8; French trans. by J. Cantineau, *Principes de Phonologie*, Paris, 1949, p. 5.

fulfils a definite function in *langue*'.[16] This last definition is a pointer to the path that phonologists have taken to find a way out of the impasse that their research seemed to be leading into. For how can one study the 'sounds of *langue*'? Phoneticians have at their disposal tangible subjects for experimentation, viz. concrete acts of speech, sounds that are uttered by individuals and that they can analyse and measure, a task that is greatly facilitated by the use of advanced laboratory techniques.

The phonologist has none of these advantages. How indeed could he, with such an abundance of precautions, study the sounds of *something that does not exist*, or, more precisely, something that does not exist in material form? In such a situation, the problem must be tackled obliquely. Given the impossibility of embarking upon a positive study of the sounds of *langue*, an attempt had to be made to proceed in a negative way by trying to describe what they are not or, more exactly, what they differ from. Phonologists have therefore resorted to the criterion of *functional* (or *distinctive* or *pertinent*) oppositions. In the system constituted by a language, a phoneme is of interest only in so far as it has a functional role. Phonologists therefore set out to discover 'what phonic differences are linked, in the language under investigation, to differences of meaning'.[17] But, by a curious paradox—especially if one bears in mind what the intention of the founders of phonology was—the science of sounds envisaged in this way has lost the character of universality that it had when it was concerned only with studying *parole*. Each language, in fact, has its own sound system and the set of oppositions forming its structure varies from one language to another. One can draw up a phonetic table of the sounds of human speech from which each language draws the elements forming its own system, but as many phonological tables must be drawn up as there are different dialects in the world.

Suppose we take the case of the opposition voiced/voiceless. Phonetics teaches us that the difference between [p] and [b] results from the fact that, when we pronounce [b], a current of air causes the thyro-artenoid muscles (the vocal cords) to vibrate as it passes through them on its way to the point of articulation at the lips. Phonology is not concerned with explanations of this kind and if it recognizes [p] and [b] as different phonemes in French this is because

---

[16] Trubetzkoy, *Grundzüge*, p. 14; French trans., pp. 11-12.
[17] Ibid.

of their differentiatory function, by virtue of the fact that this opposition allows a distinction to be made between concepts, e.g. between *poule* and *boule*, *pierre* and *bière*, *pont* and *bond*, etc., so that the phonological opposition between [p] and [b] (or more generally the opposition voiceless/voiced) has a functional yield in French. On the other hand, there are languages, such as the Polynesian group, in which the difference between voiceless and voiced has no functional value since there is not a single pair of words that it serves to distinguish.

A curious example relating to vowels is provided by Adyghe (or Lower Cherkess, a northern Caucasian dialect) which has three vocalic values, distinguished by the degree of aperture, viz. (1) a type having minimum aperture, realized as [i], [y] or [u], (2) a type having medium aperture, realized as [e], [œ] or [o], (3) a type having maximum aperture, realized as various shades of [a]. These variations within each type are conditioned by the phonetic circumstances of the vowel and the speaker is not aware of these differences in timbre. A foreigner thinks, quite correctly, that he hears [i] and [u], [e] and [o], etc., but native speakers are aware of only one important element, the degree of aperture; from the functional point of view, this is the only element that matters since, so long as the aperture remains constant, the timbre of the vowel may vary without having on that account any differentiatory value (indeed, in spelling, the Cherkesses use only three letters to represent these three vowel phonemes).[18]

To sum up, the Adyghe vowel system has three degrees of aperture that form a distinctive (i.e. functional) opposition but, within each degree of aperture, variations of timbre, being conditioned, are not interchangeable and so they form a non-distinctive opposition (or, in other words, a phonetic but not a phonological opposition). Aperture is therefore a mark of pertinent correlation whereas timbre is a non-pertinent characteristic. If one thinks of the essential role that the alternation *e/o* plays in Indo-European,[19] one can measure the extent of the difference between one type of language and another.

Without going into more technical aspects such as the procedures employed by phonology to analyse from its own point of view the

[18] Trubetzkoy, *Grundzüge*, pp. 87–88; French trans., p. 102.
[19] V. sup., p. 33.

phonic elements of language,[20] let us turn at once to the definition of the phoneme proposed by Trubetzkoy: 'The phoneme is the sum of the phonologically pertinent features of a phonic image'.[21] Thus, it can be seen that the phoneme does not coincide with a concrete phonic image but only with those of its features that help to create distinctive oppositions. Indeed, for phonemes to be recognizable, they must be distinguishable in opposition to others. Of course, once an opposition has been recognized in a language this is sufficient to individualize the phoneme even in those cases where there is no differentiatory opposition.[22]

The physiological justification for this new way of envisaging the sounds of human language is in fact to be found in the data of traditional phonetics. Language, as everyone knows, is not an organic necessity in man, as all the organs it uses have other functions—breathing and eating—that are essential to human life, but it is also true that a person who has been accidentally deprived (by malformation, paralysis or removal) of one of his speech organs can make a substitute organ by using parts of the body that do not

---

[20] The procedure known as *commutation* makes it possible to distinguish between *permutable* and *impermutable* sounds, the former occurring in the same phonetic circumstances (such as [ε] and [ɔ] in French: *sel/sol*) whereas this is not possible in the case of the latter (such as [e] and [o] in Adyghe, or [x] and [ç] in German—*doch/dich*—in which [x] occurs only after [a] or a back vowel whereas [ç] appears in all other positions but never after [a] or a back vowel). *Neutralizable* oppositions are those that have functional value only in certain positions (e.g. the French opposition between [e] and [ε] is pertinent in for example open, stressed syllables—*j'irai* [ʒire]/*j'irais* [ʒirε]—but is neutralized for in example unstressed syllables where, normally, it is conditioned, [e] occurring in open syllables and [ε] in closed syllables: *léger* [leʒe]/*lecteur* [lεktœr]). A mark of *correlation* is the element that characterizes the members of the same series and makes it possible to integrate them in pairs or correlative bundles (such as, for example, nasality in the French vowel pairs [a/ã], [ε/ε̃], [ɔ/ɔ̃] and [œ/œ̃]. The notion of *archiphoneme* by which the phonologists meant the distinctive features common to two or more correlative phonemes, apart from their correlative properties (e.g. in French the archiphoneme E includes the varieties [e], [ε] and [ε̃]), has given rise to much discussion and the difficulty of determining its range of applicability (e.g. in French, is [m] to be linked with [p] and [b] in the same archiphoneme?) has caused it to be dropped.—Cf. Trubetzkoy, *Grundzüge*, pp. 31, 69–71, 77, French trans. pp. 34, 80–82, 89; Martinet, *Économie des changements phonétiques*, pp. 70, 72–73, 100–101.

[21] Trubetzkoy, *Grundzüge*, p. 35; French trans., p. 40.

[22] So, to return to the example quoted above (pp. 66–67), the voiceless quality of [p] and the voiced quality of [b] which in French serve to differentiate between the members of each of the pairs *poule/boule, pierre/bière*, etc., are also preserved even in those cases where the distinction is not operative, as in *page, pose* on the one hand, *base, biche* on the other (there are no such words as *bage, *bose, *pase, *piche), etc.; cf. André Martinet, 'Concerning the preservation of useful sound features', in *Word*, IX, 1953, 1–11.

normally come into use in the act of speech (the folds of the oesopha-
gus, for example, may serve instead of the glottis in the case of
extirpation of the larynx): the result is speech that is of course
different but still comprehensible. These experimental data confirm
the fact that what is important in language is not the strictly accurate
utterance of the phonemes but the possibility of making use of
oppositions, for 'it is not essential that a phoneme should conform
strictly to the phoneme most widely used by the linguistic group,
but is essential that it should be sufficiently differentiated from other
phonemes used by the speaker'.[23]

Quite apart from the interest of its methods and the rules it has
laid down for descriptive procedures, phonology, which is a further
working-out of Saussurian ideas, has had the signal merit of stimu-
lating renewed thought upon linguistics. We shall see indeed that
from it have sprung the various currents that may be grouped under
the heading of 'structuralism'. But it has also opened up new perspectives for traditional comparative and historical grammar. The
analysis of the flow of speech into distinctive units brings out more
systematically the functional role of phonemes, for example in
the principle of alternation which, both on the semasiological and
on the morphological plane,[24] plays such an important role in
most languages; see, for example, the alternation of vowel timbre
in Greek λέγω/λόγος, German *Mutter/Mütter*, French *j'irai/j'irais*,
patte/pâte or, to go no farther afield than French, the formation of
the feminine of many adjectives either by the alternation voiceless/
voiced: *neuf/neuve* (/nœf/, /nœv/) or by the alternation —/+ (the addition of a consonant): *vert/verte*(/vɛr/, /vɛrt/), *grand/ grande* (/grã/,
/grãd/), etc. Together with this fundamental distinctive value of
phonemes, their use as signs of demarcation should also be noted.
Here, it is instructive to compare German and French: in German, the
phonetic word coincides with the grammatical word, but French makes
use of liaison, with however the possibility (admittedly only in very few

[23] André Ombredane, *L'aphasie et l'élaboration de la pensée explicite*, Paris, 1951, pp
282–283. He adds, 'A Marseillais and a Picard have no difficulty in understanding one
another in spite of the phonetic differences between their respective ways of speaking'.
[24] To designate the study of the way the phonological resources of a language are
used to serve morphological ends, Trubetzkoy had created the term *morphophonology* or
morphonology (*Grundzüge*, pp. 268–271; French trans., pp. 337–341). [Those English-
speaking linguists who prefer *phonemics* to *phonology* have also devised the term *morpho-
phonemics*; see for example C. F. Hockett, *A Course in Modern Linguistics*, New York,
1958, pp. 134, etc.; H. A. Gleason, *An Introduction to Descriptive Linguistics*, revised ed.,
1961, pp. 82 etc.]

F

cases) of marking a distinction by means of the presence or absence of liaison: *les héros* /le ero/ and *les zéros* /le zero /, *un savant aveugle* (without liaison, /œ̃ savɑ̃ avœgl/ 'a blind scholar') and *un savant aveugle* (with liaison, /œ̃ savɑ̃ t avœgl/ 'a learned blind man'). Even the aesthetics of language has benefited from the application of principles which will indicate how far the phonology of poetic language differs from that of the contemporary spoken language (see for example the question of the 'mute *e*' in modern French).[25]

Finally, a more recent aspect of phonology must be stressed. At first, the researches of the phonologists, preoccupied as they were with establishing the methodology of their discipline and demonstrating its usefulness, dealt essentially with states of language and that solely within the synchronic dimension. But once their position was consolidated and their technique perfected, they realized the interest of applying the methods of the new discipline to evolutionary linguistics. As a matter of fact, this possibility had been glimpsed right from the outset,[26] since *Proposition 22* of the Hague Congress states that 'the antinomy of synchronic phonology and diachronic phonetics would be done away with the moment phonetic changes were considered in function of the phonological system that they affect', and, in 1931, R. Jakobson published his *Principes de phonologie historique*.[27] These appeals met with a positive response: there will be no more histories of particular forms without reference to the system of which they are an integral part, after the fashion of the countless and indeed necessary and very valuable works of detail undertaken by the neogrammarians and their followers. The elements of a linguistic system are so closely bound up with one another that our only chance of explaining particular developments lies in considering the development of the system in itself. And so there is propounded the notion of an equilibrium which, in the course of the evolution of a language, regulates the relationships between different counterbalancing tendencies. Here again, the idea is found, right at the beginning, in *Proposition 22*: 'The problem of the purpose

---

[25] J. Vendryes, 'La phonologie et la langue poétique', in *Conférences de l'Institut de Linguistique de l'Université de Paris*, II, 1934, 39–51.

[26] As early as 1890 Paul Passy had 'set out in a few paragraphs the most lucid exposition of the functionalist theory of sound changes' (Martinet, *Économie des changements phonétiques*, pp. 42–43), but the interest of this theory was not understood at the time.

[27] *Travaux du Cercle Linguistique de Prague*, IV, 1931, 247–267; the text was reprinted in Cantineau's French translation of Trubetzkoy's *Grundzüge*, pp. 315–336.

of these changes must be raised. Thus historical phonetics is transformed into a history of the evolution of a phonological system.'
We may recall in this connection that, in view of the fact that
phonologists operated, in their diachronic work, by postulating a
certain tendency towards 'harmony' in phonological systems, it has
sometimes been alleged, very artificially, that their research was
tainted with teleology.

Yet it is only recently that phonetics and phonology have begun
to be considered as 'the two sides of the same thing', as Malmberg
puts it.[28] Diachronic phonology has really got under way since
the Second World War. It has had the particular merit of directing
its appeal at traditionalist linguists and persuading them of the
absolute necessity of setting historical phonetics in its functional
framework. One of the main promoters of this 'reconciliation'
between comparatists and phonologists has been André Martinet
whose numerous works, including a general treatise entitled
Économie des changements phonétiques[29]—we shall refer later[30] to his
Éléments de linguistique générale—, have set out the bases and general
lines on which these two branches of linguistic science can col-
laborate. The care with which the illustrative examples are chosen
and when necessary philologically discussed has greatly contributed
to winning the confidence of the comparatists.

We must make it clear that by 'economy' Martinet means the
principle of 'least effort' (or of 'least expenditure') as well as that of
internal organization thanks to which a balance is struck between
the fundamental antinomic tendencies that he observes between
'man's need to communicate and to express himself' and 'his tendency
to reduce to a minimum his mental and physical activity'. Martinet
sees too in the inertia and asymmetry of the speech organs a decisive
reason why equilibrium never results in complete symmetry; that is
why he substitutes for the 'teleological' notion of harmony envisaged
by the early phonologists that of a tendency towards stabilizing the
system by integrating the phonemes: indeed, isolated phonemes, not

[28] Bertil Malmberg's *Le système consonantique du français moderne*, Lund-Copenhagen
1943, has as its sub-title: *Études de phonologie et de phonétique*; the following year he
published an essay entitled *Die Quantität als phonetisch-phonologischer Begriff*, Lund-
Leipzig, 1944.
[29] The sub-title is *Traité de phonologie diachronique*, Berne, 1955; see especially pp.
94–104.
[30] P. 83 and n. 74.

integrated in correlations or bundles, seem somewhat unstable and tend either to disappear or to find a correlative partner.

Structuralism. It is really somewhat artificial to begin another chapter at this point, for we have already been speaking of structuralism in dealing with some aspects of phonology, and these two fields of research are closely linked. Indeed—and this marks a new stage in the exploitation of Saussurian principles—the method evolved by the phonologists for examining the system and behaviour of phonemes from a totally different angle, a method that brought into relief the parallelism between the levels of content (concept) and expression (form), has been applied to all aspects of language, language being considered as a structure made up of a network of elements each having a particular functional value. For the *structuralists* (as the members of this school of thought are known), applying the concluding formula of the *Cours*—and though not formulated by Saussure himself, this has nevertheless had profound repercussions—viz. that 'the one and only true object of linguistics is language envisaged in and for itself', and invoking the dimensional notion of linguistic segments, have made a remarkable effort to explain language in terms of itself. To do so, they have undertaken a careful examination of the relationships uniting the elements of speech (*Nothing is isolated and everything participates in everything*, as Anaxagoras said long ago), and their research has aimed at determining the functional value of these different kinds of relationships. For one of their merits, and by no means the least of them, has been to see clearly that, in the matter of language, A + B is different from B + A and that the whole is greater than the sum of its parts;[31] one need only consider the scorn with which Trubetzkoy spoke of the proponents of historical linguistics and neogrammarian phonetics, calling them 'atomists and individualists'.[32]

Saussure, in a famous image, compared language to a game of chess: 'in both we have before us a system of values, and we observe the ways in which these are modified';[33] in chess, if we move one

[31] Applying this principle to sociology, Durkheim had deduced the existence of the 'collective consciousness'; see for example R. Aron, 'La Sociologie', in *Les Sciences Sociales en France: Enseignement et Recherches*, Paris, 1937, pp. 13–48.

[32] Cf. for example 'La phonologie actuelle', in *Journal de Psychologie*, XXX, 1933, 227–246.

[33] *Cours*, p. 125.—In reality, what is modified is the network of forces and not, as É. Buyssens points out, the system itself, since each piece retains its value.

piece we change the balance of the whole network of pieces, likewise, 'language is not an aggregate of heterogeneous elements; it is an articulate system of interdependent and closely integrated units which derive their significance from their structural position'.[34]

In general, structuralists, taking no heed of the facts of evolution, have entrenched themselves resolutely in the synchronic dimension, but whereas some of them adhere to concepts inherited from general grammar, others make a clear distinction between form and substance, and others take abstraction so far that they are interested only in the system independently of its concrete manifestation. We shall indicate below, amongst the theories that have been elaborated within this current of thought, only those that have had the widest repercussions and that seem to present the greatest interest.

Harking back to the tradition of the Ancients, the Danish linguist V. Brøndal (died 1942) attempted to 'discover in language the concepts of logic, as they have been elaborated by philosophers from Aristotle to the logicians of the present day'.[35] With this end in view, he strove for example to explain the principal facts of morphological structure by reducing the categories that are their expression to fundamental relationships arranged each within a well-defined framework. Starting from the principle of functional binarism, he distinguished a *negative* and a *positive*—terms of polarity indicating of course contraries of one kind or another—such as the pairs singular/plural or preterite/present. There would also be a third term, *neutral* or zero, neither negative nor positive (such as the indicative, which is an amodal form, or the third person which is defined as being neither the first person nor the second). To these three terms—negative, positive and neutral—one could add a fourth: the *complex* which is both negative and positive, e.g., the dual which is a singular-plural, or the optative mood which combines the characters of the subjunctive and the imperative.[36] The set of terms defined in this way allows of a multiplicity of combinations which, in Brøndal's view, could form the basis of morphological systems.

[34] S. Ullmann, *Précis de sémantique française*, 2nd ed., Berne, 1959, p. 26.

[35] Viggo Brøndal, *Essais de linguistique générale*, Copenhagen, 1943, p. x.

[36] The fact that the imperative is included amongst the moods indicates, in our view, how forced the operation is. We consider that the imperative stands apart as a form belonging to affective or expressive language which is outside the normal pattern of the modal category, just as the vocative does not form part of the case system of nouns (as is shown, on the genetic plane, by the very form—the simple stem—of both).

The rigorous logic with which Brøndal constructed his theory by fitting the facts into pre-established patterns of a binary type has also attracted other scholars. The basis of Mikuš's syntagmatics, for example, is the analysis of an utterance that is divided up more or less artificially in order to obtain binary structures.[37] R. Jakobson, one of the founders of phonology (and we are not leaving the topic of structuralism by reverting for a moment to that of phonology) and the leader of the 'Harvard school', conceives of the distinctive units of language as combinations of features in strictly binary relationships, the pertinent oppositions observed in the languages of the world being reduced to twelve binary oppositions, at least some of which, it is suggested, are found in any linguistic system.[38] So, over against the flexible system proposed by Trubetzkoy who distinguished between correlative and disjunctive oppositions, Jakobson propounds a radical binarism. But it must be recognized that in order to arrive at such a presentation of the facts some features must be considered as essential and relevant to the establishment of the schema whilst others must be left out of account as secondary or 'redundant'.[39] We are therefore brought back to the primordial question that every linguist comes up against in attempting to make a classification, whatever the plan of his research, namely that of choosing and evaluating criteria: which facts are relevant, how can their importance be assessed, how can one avoid arbitrariness? As Martinet has said, 'it must be repeated yet again that it is not up to language to conform to the edicts of linguists, it is up to linguists to adapt their methods if they do not do full justice to the language being studied'.[40]

Thinking along similar lines to Brøndal, the French linguist, G. Guillaume, made a name for himself with his penetrating studies on the category of the verb and on the problem of the article in

[37] Francis Mikuš, 'Quelle est en fin de compte la structure-type du langage?' in *Lingua*, III, 1953, 340–370; 'En marge du Sixième Congrès International des Linguistes' (à propos of syntagmatics) in *Miscelánea homenaje a André Martinet*, Vol. I, La Laguna, 1957, 159–221.
[38] Roman Jakobson, Gunnar Fant and Morris Halle, *Preliminaries to Speech Analysis: The distinctive features and their correlates*, Cambridge, Mass., 1952; Roman Jakobson and Morris Halle, *Fundamentals of Language*, The Hague, 1956.
[39] See Martinet's constructive criticism, *Économie des changements phonétiques*, pp. 73–77.
[40] Ibid., pp. 125–126.

French. As an avowed follower of Saussurian teaching,[41] he tried to create what he called psycho-systematics (*la psycho-systématique*), a new part of linguistics that would be devoted to the study of systems. Although he claimed that his doctrine was strictly orthodox, in the tradition of Meillet, Guillaume made a vigorous attack on traditional positivist linguistics which, by trying to adhere too closely to reality, 'debars itself *ipso facto* from seeing it as a whole, as reality extends far beyond what is directly observable'. In fact, psycho-systematics studies the ways in which series of morphemes are integrated. Now, if morphemes can be studied pragmatically in speech, the same is not true of systems that are accessible only via a process of thought that is beyond the scope of directly ascertainable facts. Systems have in fact no *signifiants*, or none that represent them in their entirety; that is, they are beyond the reach of direct observation and are accessible, as the author himself states, only via an alliance 'of shrewd observation of the concrete and of profound abstract reflection'. The result is the paradoxical situation that a book devoted to the study of Greek and Latin grammatical forms (it dealt with the formation of the time image in the classical languages) took the form of an exposé without examples 'as the phenomenon described existed in the mind prior to the formation of any examples'.[42] The work of Guillaume (who died in 1960) is loyally carried on in the writings of R. Valin[43] who also rejects the 'excessively positivist' conception of traditional linguistics and resorts to a logico-geometric language (processes of thought being represented in diagrammatic form) to expound the subtleties of 'psycho-mechanics' (*la psychomécanique*).

But the most vigorous structuralist theory and the one that has been worked out in the greatest detail and has had the greatest repercussions whilst at the same time giving rise to the greatest amount of reservation is beyond doubt the Danish linguist Hjelmslev's *glossematics*. Though the word itself goes back to 1936, the theory which was first outlined in 1928 and has since been carried

---

[41] Cf. for example Gustave Guillaume, *La langue est-elle ou n'est-elle pas un système?* Quebec, 1952, p. 4.
[42] G. Guillaume, *L'architectonique du temps dans les langues classiques*, Copenhagen, 1945, especially pp. 11–15, 17 and 65, n. 1.
[43] Roch Valin, *Petite introduction à la psychomécanique du langage*, Quebec, 1954.

further in numerous works on points of detail[44] has not yet been the subject of a complete overall exposition.[45] The very choice of this new term is a clear indication that the author, when constructing his theory, wished to make in some sort a clean sweep of pre-existing speculations, with the obvious exception of those of Saussure. Glossematics, which aims at making linguistic science fully independent of all subjective appraisal, seeks to establish a kind of algebra of language, i.e. a network of definitions forming a system that can serve as a model for the description of particular languages.

Hjelmslev (who died in 1965), considering language as a self-sufficient whole possessing a structure *sui generis*, lays great stress on the Saussurian distinction 'language is form and not substance',[46] stating explicitly that 'linguistic form is independent of the substance in which it appears. The only way one can recognize and define form is to look at it from the point of view of function.'[47] In other words, substance, so long as it has not been structuralized, remains an amorphous mass, a nebula as Saussure would have said.[48] The structure of a language is defined by Hjelmslev as 'a network of dependences or, to put it more exactly, more technically and more simply, a network of functions'.[49] More recently, he proposed the following definition: 'A structure is an autonomous entity of internal dependences'.[50] There is a clear intention to 'reduce the system of formal logic and that of language to a common principle that could be called a sublogical system'.[51]

[44] See Louis Hjelmslev, *Essais linguistiques*, Copenhagen, 1959 (=*Travaux du Cercle Linguistique de Copenhague*, XII), a volume of 15 selected articles that best reflect the evolution of the author's thought in the field of general linguistics.

[45] Only one volume appeared of the series *Outline of Glossematics: A Study in the Methodology of the Humanities with Special Reference to Linguistics*, in which Louis Hjelmslev and H. J. Uldall (both now dead) collaborated and which was intended to expound the bases and applications of the new discipline. This first volume which, apart from Hjelmslev's preface, was written by Uldall, is entitled *General Theory* (=*Travaux du Cercle Linguistique de Copenhague*, X).—The study of glossematics can best be approached through B. Siertsema's *A Study of Glossematics: Critical Survey of its Fundamental Concepts*, The Hague, 1955, (2nd ed., 1965), and Henning Spang-Hanssen's 'Glossematics' in *Trends in European and American Linguistics, 1930–1960* (v. sup. p. vii), 128–164.

[46] *Cours*, p. 169.   [47] *Bulletin du Cercle Linguistique de Copenhague*, IV, 1939, 3–4.
[48] V. inf., p. 92.
[49] 'La notion de rection' in *Acta Linguistica*, I, 1939, 11 (=*Essais linguistiques*, p. 140).
[50] *Proceedings of the Eighth International Congress of Linguists*, Oslo, 1958, p. 641.
[51] On these relationships between language and logic, cf. Leo Apostel, 'Logique et langage considérés du point de vue de la précorrection des erreurs', in L. Apostel, B. Mandelbrot and A. Morf, *Logique, langage et théorie de l'information*, Paris, 1957, especially pp. 135–151.

We must not close our eyes to the danger of such theories or underestimate the errors of judgment they may give rise to. Devoting one's attention to the system in itself without reference to its concrete realization leads to abstract constructions that the slightest flaw in our reasoning can transform into artificial speculations having no connection with the tangible bases of our knowledge.

With the praiseworthy intention of rendering his views more precise and of giving as clear a picture as possible of them, Hjelmslev also created a special terminology that gives his work a hermetic appearance and makes it most disconcerting to read for the uninitiated. Indeed, his work can only be understood when once one has fully grasped a whole set of esoteric terms of which some are quite new, like *pleremes* and *cenemes* (the former being the elements on the level of content, the latter on the level of expression),[52] or *functive* (qualifying the two terms of a function), whilst others are familiar words used with an unusual meaning, such as *function* which means 'the relationship between two functives', or *relation* (= the *function* 'both—and'), *correlation* (= the *function* 'either—or'), etc.

Such procedures run the risk of encouraging a certain verbalism that could easily be substituted for knowledge acquired by direct contact with reality. Of course, there was no such danger for Hjelmslev who did not hazard theoretical views on language without first going deeply into its different aspects and mastering the philological and linguistic technique. Likewise, Guillaume, when he affirms that structure is immanent in language as it is actually realized and defines his method as an alliance of observation of the concrete and of abstract reflection, is careful to make it clear that observation has of course the last word since it alone is 'qualified to decide ultimately what is the true nature of things, the role of reflection in its alliance with observation being not to come to conclusions in its place but to guide it, to make it more acute, more penetrating, and, in a word, to confer upon it a power which, left to itself, it would not have'.[53] But what is to be feared—and this is a fear that is confirmed by the facts—is that over-zealous disciples, unconsciously carried away by formulae that they have neither devised nor tested themselves, will substitute for solid and fruitful linguistic reflection

[52] These are therefore not the same as the 'empty words' and 'full words' referred to by the Chinese grammarians (cf. sup., p. 18).

[53] *L'architectonique du temps* (cf. sup. p. 75, n. 42), p. 17.

a flood of speculation that is devoid of tangible foundations and therefore purely artificial. It is somewhat perturbing to find, for example, some American linguists speaking of a *metalinguistics*—or of an *exolinguistics*—which would deal solely with relationships and leave phonetics to physicists and semantics to sociologists.[54]

Another, and much more real and more serious, danger is that in these systematic constructions that are erected with the rigour of logico-mathematical theories and often by means of algebraic-like formulae, language tends to be considered as a datum, as a being in its own right detached from human contingencies (Hjelmslev goes so far as to claim that, language being an abstract entity, the system is independent of its concrete manifestation)[55] and, by a return to conceptions that were in favour last century and that one might have thought to be quite out of date,[56] linguistics is again being assimilated to the natural or so-called exact sciences. One comes to the point of reasoning and speculating not on the basis of facts and the various aspects they offer to direct observation, but on the basis of deductions drawn from their existence, on the basis of schemes that it has been thought possible to draw up according to their reciprocal relationship within the system. In other words, linguistics thought of in this way becomes strangely remote from this essentially human, living and multiform thing that language is, and is in danger of turning into a formalist conceptualism confined within the field of intellectual speculation. It is not without reason that the structuralists have been reproached with being all too often way up in the stratosphere and not bothering about the concrete realities that are the very substance of our science.[57]

And so we arrive at the paradox that linguistic theories that were first worked out in a sociological spirit and in consideration of the close relationships between language and society have led some researchers to a stage strangely remote from the initial conception.

[54] Cf. for example Einar Haugen, 'Directions in modern linguistics', in *Language*, XXVII, 1951, 221–222; J. B. Carroll, *The Study of Language: A survey of linguistics and related disciplines in America*, Cambridge, Mass., 1954.—In applied linguistics, the term *metalinguistics* is applied to the formulation of grammatical frameworks (for natural or artificial languages) with a view to their use by 'translating machines' (v. inf., p. 81). Here too, then, such a level of abstraction is adopted that all contact with the concrete is lost.

[55] Cf. for example B. Malmberg in *Studia linguistica*, III, 1949, 132; V. Kopal in *Lingua*, II, 1950, 231–232.

[56] V. sup., p. 16.

[57] J. Orr in *Actes du sixième Congrès International des Linguistes*, Paris, 1949, pp. lxiii–lxv.

For Saussure was certainly impregnated with the sociological spirit. 'All the avenues of his teaching bring us back to the consideration of language as a social fact. . . . After reading his book, one carries away with one the clear impression that linguistics is essentially a sociological science.' Doubtless, Saussurian thought is deeply marked also by the psychological point of view, but this judgment on the sociological direction of the *Cours*, written by J. Vendryes in 1921,[58] is on the whole valid. Now it scarcely seems possible to imagine theories further removed from social realities than the purely abstract speculations that some structuralists go in for (we are now referring only to those who take up the most extreme positions).

This doctrinaire tendency is not of course confined to linguistics, for the urge to systematize invades all the sciences. We find it not only in related disciplines such as philology, history, archaeology, the history of religions, and so on, but also in others which, founded as they are on the experimental method, might at first sight seem less prone to accidents of this kind. Thus it is that Cuvier's systematism dominated zoology in France at the beginning of the nineteenth century in spite of sharp criticism from such clear-sighted scholars as Geoffroy-Saint-Hilaire. E. Janssens has rightly pointed out in this connection that the fact that scholasticism revives 'every time a school of thought tries to impose its scientific theories by force of formal logic rather than by observable experiment is proof that conceptualism is one of the most active motive forces in human thought and that the scientist must be continually striving to keep it within bounds'.[59]

Nevertheless, if the systematization preached by certain structuralists seems to go too far, it is only fair to recognize that some kind of systematization had become indispensable and so it is not surprising that such currents of thought have appeared in the study of linguistics. The complexity and immensity of a matter as rich and as fugitive as human speech had resulted in a considerable body of research on particular points of detail but these studies, which had revealed the extent of the investigation that had to be undertaken

---

[58] 'Le caractère social du langage et la doctrine de F. de Saussure', in *Journal de Psychologie*, XVIII, 1941, 624 (=*Choix d'études linguistiques et celtiques*, Paris, 1952, p. 25).
[59] É. Janssens, 'Platon et les sciences d'observation', in *Revue de l'Université de Bruxelles*, II, 1949–1950, 266.

and the fields that had to be explored, were uncoordinated and often evinced a singular dearth of general ideas. It is therefore understandable that some theorists, hoping to facilitate the work of researchers by suggesting certain guiding principles, should have yielded to the pressing need to make, sometimes prematurely, a synthesis of the multifarious aspects of language, to cast light where confusion seemed to reign and that consequently they should have been attracted by metaphysical-looking conceptions and, in order to describe the objects of their science with greater precision, have adopted the methods of symbolic logic. Guillaume's psycho-systematics was heading in this direction but, as we have seen, he was able to rely on a solid basis of precise knowledge of the linguistic facts.

Some American linguists on the other hand have gone much further and indulged in speculations that are divorced from reality. The analytical method of Z. S. Harris for example is a logico-mathematical construction lacking firm foundation.[60] He deliberately restricted his research to questions of distribution, i.e. to the freedom with which the different elements occur relatively to one another, and he does this in turn for the phonic and the morphological elements, thereby eliminating the meaning of words from his analysis, as B. Bloch and G. Trager had done before him.[61] One wonders what happens, with this purely mechanical procedure, when the criterion of distribution is considered to be the only relevant one, to the expressive, stylistic and other variants that are of prime importance in communication amongst human beings. The method is all the less convincing since the philological facts that Harris quotes do not always seem to be well established and give the impression that the author adapts them to fit the needs of his argument.[62] A further condemnation of the method is the fact that Harris and those of his colleagues who adopt it, applying it to various fields but in particular to one that is as well known and has been as thoroughly studied as present-day English, arrive at differing

[60] Zellig S. Harris, *Structural Linguistics*, 2nd ed., Chicago, 1960 (the 1st edition had appeared in 1951 under the title *Methods in Structural Linguistics*).

[61] Bernard Bloch and George Trager, *Outline of Linguistic Analysis*, Baltimore, 1942.

[62] See J. Cantineau's severe criticism in *Bulletin de la Société de Linguistique de Paris*, L, fasc. 2, 1954, 4–9.

results and modify their conclusions from one experiment to another.[63]

Statistics and the calculation of probabilities have obviously played a prominent part in this mathematical formulation of linguistic description[64] and N. Chomsky, in particular, has undertaken a far-reaching analysis of grammatical structure by working out a formalization of linguistic levels according to the methods of formal logic.[65] Studies such as these have proved extremely valuable for the practical purposes of language-teaching. They are also at the basis of applied linguistics, one of whose most spectacular achievements, brought about by the collaboration of linguists with mathematicians and technicians, is undoubtedly the development of machine translation.[66] Work on these lines has gone ahead particularly in Russia and the English-speaking countries, but as yet the methods are far from perfect and have been applied only to technical languages. The regrettable thing is that the use of these mathematical methods, of which no one would deny the legitimacy and the utility, once again obscures the real nature of linguistics. J. Whatmough's *Language*, a lively and original work, which oddly combines humanist reminiscences with unveiled admiration for technological achievements such as electronic computers,[67] sets out, it would appear, to show that linguistics is to be classified amongst the natural sciences, and B. Mandelbrot, at the conclusion of an excellent programme article on the possibility of applying the concepts of communication theory to the study of language, expresses the hope that it will not be long before 'the study of language will once and for all break through the imaginary barrier

---

[63] See in this connection Einar Haugen's remarks, 'Directions in Modern Linguistics', in *Language*, XXVII, 1951, p. 219 and n. 29.

[64] Cf. Warren Plath, 'Mathematical Linguistics', in *Trends in European and American Linguistics, 1930–1960* (cf. sup., p. vii) pp. 21–57; see also below p. 140 and n. 248.

[65] Cf. Noam Chomsky, 'The Logical Basis of Linguistic Theory', in *Proceedings of the Ninth International Congress of Linguists* (Cambridge, Mass., 1962), The Hague, 1964, pp. 914–987; *Current Issues in Linguistic Theory*, The Hague, 1964.

[For a detailed exposition of Chomsky's theory of transformational grammar, see his two fundamental books, *Syntactic Structures*, The Hague, 1957, and *Aspects of the Theory of Syntax*, Cambridge, Mass., 1965; see also Z. S. Harris, *String Analysis of Sentence Structure*, The Hague, 1962, and E. Bach, *An Introduction to Transformational Grammars*, New York, 1964.]

[66] Cf. G. Mounin, *Les problèmes théoriques de la traduction*, Paris, 1963, and *La Machine à traduire*, The Hague, 1964.

[67] Joshua Whatmough, *Language: a Modern Synthesis*, London, 1956 (paperback ed., New York, 1957).

82   LINGUISTICS IN THE TWENTIETH CENTURY

that has hitherto separated it from the exact sciences': the old
Schleicherian myth dies hard![68]

But some have gone even further than this. Linguistic statistics,
the scope of which was at first restricted to the synchronic description of languages—and even in this sphere there are considerable
fluctuations and the results are dependent on too many subjective
factors[69]—has been extended to diachrony in the form of *glotto-
chronology*, advocated principally by Morris Swadesh[70] and later
rechristened *lexicostatistics*. The aim of this method is to calculate,
on the basis of a study of vocabulary (it is claimed that the rate at
which words are replaced by others in the course of time follows a
constant rhythm represented by a certain percentage over a period
of a thousand years), the date when two or more related languages
separated. It is disappointing to observe that this method, which
it is true was evolved for the purpose of studying and classifying
Amerindian languages, i.e. languages that have no history, proves
to be completely false when applied to languages that have a history,
such as the Romance languages. In the latter case the results obtained
by lexicostatistical methods are unacceptable and in flagrant contradiction to the facts.[71]

However, there has been a salutary reaction on the part of some
linguists who are sympathetic to the structuralist trend but are
anxious not to be carried away by a sterile and gratuitous intellec-
tualism. We have already shown[72] how Martinet, thanks to his
realistic approach to diachronic phonology, has very felicitously

[68] Benoît Mandelbrot, 'Structure formelle des textes et communication', in *Word*,
X, 1954, 1–27.—And this type of attitude is spreading: 'Linguistics, at least in several
aspects, is evolving from a humanity into a science. There is a growing recognition of
languages as natural phenomena whose secrets may yield to methods of analysis and
description akin to those that have proved fruitful in the physical sciences'—beginning
of the article 'Linguistics and Mathematics' by Anthony G. Oettinger, in *Studies presented
to Joshua Whatmough*, The Hague, 1957, p. 179.

[69] G. Herdan's manual of linguistic statistics, *Language as Choice and Chance*, Groningen,
1956, met with a cautious welcome, in view of the insufficiency of information; it nevertheless contains some interesting indications such as the difference between the statistics
of language, which is subject to the chance constraints imposed by society, and the
statistics of style, in which the speaker's own choice intervenes.

[70] Cf. for example S. C. Gudschinsky, 'The ABC's of Lexicostatistics (Glotto-
chronology)', in *Word*, XII, 1956, 175–210; Ar. Dall'Igna Rodrigues, 'Eine neue Datie-
rungsmethode der vergleichenden Sprachwissenschaft', in *Kratylos*, II, 1957, 1–13.

[71] Cf. Eugenio Coseriu, 'Critique de la glottochronologie appliquée aux langues
romanes', in *Actes du Xe Congrès International de Linguistique et Philologie Romanes* (*Strasbourg, 1962*), Paris, 1965, I, 85–94.

[72] P. 71.

bridged the gap between traditional comparative grammar and the new conceptions, and it is well worth quoting his statement that 'it is high time that linguists became aware of the independence of their discipline and got rid of the inferiority complex that impels them to relate every step they take to some great philosophical principle; in this way they only succeed in blurring the contours of reality instead of sharpening them'.[73] In his recent *Éléments de linguistique générale*[74] he insists, and rightly, on the need to establish a liaison between pure speculation and the exploitation of the data so as to strike a balance—'more realism and less formalism'— between theory and practice.

It should also be stressed that Hjelmslev, by emphasizing function, brought out what was most fruitful in his research, and in 1929 H. Frei spoke of *functional linguistics* in opposition to both historical linguistics and normative grammar[75] and many still prefer to use this term. E. Buyssens, in a work[76] in which he attempts to integrate linguistics within semiology as it had been conceived of by Saussure[77] and expresses the view that this appellation 'sums up perfectly the point of view of what is known as structural linguistics', emphasizes that here as in every science the idea of function is the fundamental idea and consequently he studies speech (*le discours*) as 'the functional part of *parole*'. 'Function' is of course taken in the broad sense of 'the way the linguistic elements are used', and this is also how it is understood by Martinet, for whom phonology is essentially a functional discipline,[78] and the American linguist L. Bloomfield whom it is not inappropriate to mention here although he does not refer explicitly to Saussure, and his followers go so far as to deny that he was in any way influenced by Saussure;[79] Bloomfield's *Language*, that we shall return to later,[80] whilst adhering

---

[73] *Économie des changements phonétiques*, p. 18.

[74] Paris, 1960.—Cf. too his recent book *La linguistique synchronique*, Paris, 1965 (=Vol. 1 of the series *Le linguiste*), in which some of his earlier writings are reprinted.

[75] H. Frei, *La Grammaire des fautes*, Geneva, 1929, pp. 17-31.

[76] É. Buyssens, *Les langages et le discours*, Brussels, 1943, which deals on the one hand with systems of signs that act as means of communication amongst men, and on the other with the rules that govern the way they operate; cf. 'La conception fonctionnelle des faits linguistiques', in *Journal de Psychologie*, 1950, 37-53; the same author has also studied the relationships between psychology and linguistics and between thought and language, cf. for example *Revue de l'Institut de Sociologie*, 1960, 269-294.

[77] V. sup., p. 51.

[78] Cf., for example, 'Où en est la phonologie?' in *Lingua*, I, 1948, 34-58.

[79] Cf. André Martinet, *Structural Linguistics* (v. inf., n. 81), p. 577.

[80] Pp. 98 and 116.

to positivist conceptions like those of the neogrammarians, insists, in the field of static description (the only field that interests him), on the importance of functions.

We see then that the attempts made to arrive at an understanding of linguistic structure have been many and varied and that the now widely-used label of *structuralism* covers in reality, in Europe and America, a number of sometimes widely differing tendencies.[81] As Benveniste puts it, 'structure is one of the essential terms of modern linguistics, one of those that still have programmatic value'.[82] So, scholars use the word in various senses (we have either a system that explains the way a whole is arranged in interdependent parts or else the fitting together of the elements of the concrete substance into an organized whole) and, on the methodological plane, they reach conclusions that are just as varied. On the one hand the European structuralists, and above all the glossematicians, consider form as essential and as the only thing that is relevant from the linguistic point of view, so that substance is explained deductively in relation to form; on the other hand the American structuralists analyse the elements of the concrete substance and, defining them in relation to the whole into which they are organized, seek to discover the structure by an inductive method.

It is in any case undeniable that since the 1940s structuralism (or functionalism) has more than any other movement captured the attention of linguists and so, willy nilly, has become the driving force behind contemporary linguistics. Structuralism, which is an attempt to rethink the problems rather than a struggle against traditional linguistics as is sometimes said by an oversimplification, is in the forefront of modern linguistics and this is no cause for regret. It has contributed powerfully to giving specialists a taste for general ideas and showing them that theoretical views are both useful and necessary as guides to research. The consideration of the data from a strictly synchronic point of view has made it possible

---

[81] These different tendencies have been lucidly discussed by É. Benveniste in the *Journal de Psychologie*, 1954, 130–145, under the title 'Tendances récentes en linguistique générale'. André Martinet's brief but clear overall survey, 'Structural Linguistics', in the volume *Anthropology Today*, edited by A. L. Kroeber, Chicago, 1953, 574–580, may also be consulted with profit. See also B. Malmberg's clearly set out and richly documented *Structural Linguistics and Human Communication*, Berlin-Göttingen-Heidelberg, 1963 (=*Kommunikation und Kybernetik in Einzeldarstellungen*, vol. 2).

[82] 'Tendances récentes', p. 136.—Cf. the same author's *Coup d'œil sur le développement de la linguistique*, Académie des Inscriptions et Belles-Lettres, Paris, Année 1962, No. 40.

to 'isolate the purely linguistic facts independent of the changing needs of man which at every moment require adaptations of the linguistic tool'.[83] The fact that especial attention has been paid to the system has palliated the dissipation of effort that had resulted from too great a concern for detail and excessive scrupulousness in dealing with the basic data, so that gradually the gap between traditionalists and structuralists is being closed. It is structuralism, too, that has stimulated the renewal of semantics[84] and that will perhaps make possible a new departure in the field of typology.[85]

If there has been, and indeed still is, a certain overemphasis on logical rigorousness in some quarters, with the consequent danger that doctrinaire positions may again be taken up, it will also be agreed that theoretical views, at least by way of working hypotheses, have shown themselves to be fruitful and even indispensable. For the same is true of linguistics as of the human sciences in general: their bases can be discovered and the various phenomena profitably analysed only according to some guiding principle, but, on pain of falling into *a priori* and arbitrary considerations, the method must be continually tested and, if necessary, revised in function of the tangible data provided by the invigorating contribution of experience and factual observation.

The sign and its arbitrary nature. One of Saussure's most controversial ideas was his definition of the arbitrary nature of the sign. We may complete our earlier remarks by quoting in full an essential passage of the *Cours*: 'The word *arbitrary* also calls for comment. It does not imply that the *signifiant* depends on the speaker's own free choice (we shall see that the individual is powerless to modify the sign in any way at all once it is firmly established in a linguistic community). We mean that it is *unmotivated*, i.e. arbitrary in relation to the *signifié* with which it has no natural connection in actual reality.'[86] An article published by Benveniste[87] in 1939 sparked off

---

[83] André Martinet, *Éléments de linguistique générale*, Paris, 1960, p. 6; English translation by Elisabeth Palmer, *Elements of General Linguistics*, London, 1964, p. 12.

[84] V. inf., pp. 133–140.

[85] V. inf., pp. 120–132.

[86] *Cours*, p. 101; v. sup., pp. 50–52.

[87] 'Nature du signe linguistique', in *Acta Linguistica*, I, 1939, 23–29.

G

a discussion on this definition in which a number of linguists[88] have taken part and which has at times been somewhat confused because of difficulties of vocabulary: differences of terminology have on the whole been more serious than disagreements on principles. Benveniste pointed out that Saussure's reasoning 'is falsified by his unconscious and surreptitious recourse to a third term that was not included in the initial definition. This term is the thing itself, the reality'; now we must see how language is defined: 'If we accept—correctly—the principle that language is *form* not *substance*,[89] we have to admit—and Saussure clearly stated this— that linguistics is the science of forms exclusively. . . . Therefore there is a contradiction between the way Saussure defines the linguistic sign and the fundamental nature he attributes to it.'[90] To this N. Ege objected that it was quite clearly not the intention of the *Cours* to take the term *signifié* in the sense of 'thing signified', since Saussure 'did not deal with the problem, which has to do with the theory of knowledge, of the relationship between the linguistic sign and the world around us'[91] and, to account for the inconsistency noted by Benveniste, he attempted an explanation that is as unconvincing as it is subtle: 'In my view, the passage can only be understood in the following way: "We mean that the *signifiant* is unmotivated, i.e. arbitrary in relation to the *signifié* with which it [the *signifiant*] has no natural connection in actual reality", so that "it" refers to "the *signifiant*" of the preceding context (four lines above, it is true)'.[92]

If we have dwelt at some length on this controversy, the reason is that its disturbing character has recently been realized. What authorized and justified Benveniste's criticism and embarrassed those who took the opposite line was, essentially, the last part of the

---

[88] In particular, E. Lerch, A. Sechehaye, Ch. Bally, H. Frei, É. Buyssens, A. H. Gardiner and P. Naert. The situation is very well reviewed in N. Ege's article 'Le signe linguistique est arbitraire', in *Recherches structurales* (Copenhagen, 1949 =*Travaux du Cercle Linguistique de Copenhague*, V), pp. 11–29; more recently, cf. André Martinet, 'Arbitraire linguistique et double articulation', in *Cahiers Ferdinand de Saussure*, XV, 1957, 105–116; É. Buyssens, 'Le structuralisme et l'arbitraire du signe', in *Studii şi Cercetări Lingvistice*, X, 1960 (=*Omagiu lui A. Graur*), 403–416. The previously unpublished Saussuriana that have recently come to light have been turned to account in particular by R. Engler, 'Théorie et critique d'un principe saussurien: l'arbitraire du signe' (v. sup., p. 63, n. 6) and G. Lepschy, 'Ancora su "l'arbitraire du signe",' in *Annali della Scuola Normale di Pisa*, s. II, vol. XXXI, 1962, 65–102.

[89] *Cours*, pp. 157, 169.   [90] 'Nature du signe linguistique', p. 24.
[91] 'Le signe linguistique est arbitraire,' p. 19.   [92] Ibid., p. 15.

paragraph in the *Cours* where it is stated that the *signifiant* is 'arbitrary in relation to the *signifié*, with which it has no *natural* connection *in actual reality*' (our italics) (*avec lequel il n'a aucune attache* naturelle dans la réalité). The recent study of the manuscript sources of the *Cours* shows clearly that, in the passage under attack, (1) if *naturel* does not figure as an attributive adjective relating to *attache* (one passage reads: *avec lequel il n'a aucune attache première*), it does occur in a note book, but in a totally different context: *Mais le langage et l'écriture ne sont pas fondés sur un rapport naturel des choses*; (2) the expression *dans la réalité* is not attested in any of the manuscript versions of the *Cours* and is therefore one of the additions introduced by the editors in their keenness to 'render explicit' the master's thought.[93] So this lengthy discussion, however instructive and profitable it may have been, was in a sense a false problem at the outset. It is none the less true that the hesitations and indeed contradictions of the recently discovered note books reveal that on certain points Saussure's thinking had not yet crystallized and his concepts were vague and imprecise. As for the particular case just mentioned, it has to be admitted that 'a certain ambiguity subsists in the fundamental notions of sign, arbitrariness and value. It is up to linguists of the Saussurian school to follow the example of Bally and Sechehaye and grasp the master's thought, if not in its definitive at least in its most profound form.'[94]

Langue and parole. This fundamental distinction of Saussure's is now classic since it has become axiomatic and a part of standard linguistic terminology and the terms *langue* and *parole* are now normally employed in linguistic discussion in French in the sense in which they were defined by Saussure. But there has been opposition in certain quarters, and some linguists do not hesitate to speak of the 'pseudo-problems created by de Saussure's fatal dichotomy between "la parole" and "la langue"'.[95]

In fact, the root of the trouble was the oversharp distinction that Saussure seemed to draw between these two aspects of language,

---

[93] Cf. R. Godel, *Les sources manuscrites* (v. sup., p. 63, n. 5); R. Engler, in *Kratylos*, IV, 1959, 130–131.

[94] R. Godel, 'Nouveaux documents saussuriens. Les cahiers E. Constantin', in *Cahiers Ferdinand de Saussure*, XVI, 1958–1959, p. 32.

[94] L. R. Pelmer, *The Latin Language*, London, 1954, p. 195.

whereas in reality he himself, as we have already emphasized[96]—but the fact has sometimes been lost sight of—had toned down the distinction by recognizing that the two are closely linked and that *parole* is the driving force behind *langue*. From various sides, it has been proposed that a third element should be brought in, namely usage or the norm, but one must beware of the terminological difficulties created by words that are used in different senses by different authors. Hjelmslev, for example, thinks it possible to conceive of language in three different ways: the *schema*, i.e. the pure form the elements of which are defined by their oppositional, relative and negative value, *usage* or the whole set of linguistic habits which finds its concrete realization in speech acts, and the *norm*, an abstraction drawn from usage by a methodological procedure. Leaving out of account the norm, he proposes an essential distinction between schema and usage and substitutes it for the opposition between *langue* and *parole*.[97]

Coseriu on the other hand speaks of the norm as playing an intermediate role between *langue* and *parole*. The norm, representing a first degree of abstraction, consists of *parole* minus its individual and occasional variants, whilst *langue* (which he calls the 'system') represents a second degree of abstraction that retains the indispensable norms, the functional oppositions and eliminates what is merely non-distinctive tradition.[98] To take the case of vowel quantity in French, it has no function in the system (no pair of words is differentiated by vowel length), it is a characteristic of the norm (e.g. stressed /ɛ/, /ɔ/, /a/ and some other vowels are 'long' before /r/, /v/, /vr/, /z/ or /ʒ/ but generally speaking 'short' elsewhere, *mère* [mɛːr]/ *mette* [mɛt]) and it can be realized in various ways in the different individual usages that characterize *parole*.

The fact remains that in the problem of the relationships between *langue* and *parole* as defined in the *Cours* there is a fundamental aporia the solution of which appears to be beyond the reach of linguists. *Langue* in fact is not a datum to which we have direct access. It is only by considering facts of *parole* as actualizations of *langue* that we can form an idea of this abstraction. On the other hand, *parole*

[96] P. 55.

[97] Hjelmslev, 'Langue et parole', in *Cahiers Ferdinand de Saussure*, II, 1942, 29–44 (= *Essais Linguistiques*, pp. 69–81).

[98] E. Coseriu, *Sistema, Norma y Habla*, Montevideo, 1952 (reprinted in the volume *Teoria del lenguaje y lingüística general*, Madrid, 1962).

is only intelligible in so far as we can refer to *langue*, as Saussure made perfectly clear when he said that *langue* is both the instrument and the product of *parole*.[99] We see therefore that on the one hand we have concrete acts of communication and on the other a non-concrete system of signals obtained by inference from the concrete acts of communication. It is by appealing to communication theory and to the procedures of encoding and decoding used in constructing artificial languages and translating machines that L. Apostel hopes to arrive at a synthesis that would be interpreted according to the laws of logic and would account for the relationships between *langue* and *parole*.[100] But it is to be feared that such a method, relating as it does, for obvious reasons of descriptive technique, to the formal characters of the systems under study, would leave some of the most characteristic aspects of human language unaccounted for.

Synchrony and diachrony. This antinomy that played a great part in the doctrine of the *Cours* and has exercised a decisive influence on the formation of disciplines such as phonology and structuralism undoubtedly now seems one of the weakest points in Saussure's teaching. To grasp the importance that he attached to it, we must go back to the period when he was delivering his lectures and when all linguistic research—i.e. in practice comparative grammar[101]— was centred on the historical aspect. Coming from an innovator like Saussure, such a declaration on the incompatibility of diachronic and synchronic studies must surely be understood as a challenging statement of policy, couched in an extreme form designed to shake up indifference and provoke a salutary reaction.

Not much of it remains. The most forceful attack on this conception was made by the Romance philologist W. von Wartburg, a Swiss, who maintained that linguistics must do away with the gap between descriptive science and historical science. 'Linguistics in the future,' he writes, 'must seek to reach a stage at which the two points of view will be organically united so that it can be clearly seen how system and movement exert a mutual influence on one

---

[99] V. sup., p. 55.

[100] L. Apostel, 'Linguistique, théorie de la communication et logique', in *Acta Oto-Rhino-Laryngologica Belgica*, 1954, 167–189.

[101] The first chapter of the *Cours* (pp. 13–19) is entitled *Coup d'œil sur l'histoire de la linguistique*; in fact, it deals—and could only deal—with comparative grammar.

another.'[102] The distinction preached by Saussure is, in fact, essentially a methodological problem, as the opposition is in the point of view of the observer and not in the matter itself. A fact in itself is neither synchronic or diachronic, but it may be looked at from either the synchronic or the diachronic point of view. As Coseriu felicitously puts it, language functions synchronically and is constituted diachronically.[103]

Sechehaye for his part envisages a different distribution of the task, starting from the *Cours* but complementing Saussure's own views.[104] Alongside synchronic linguistics which studies the evolution of *langue*, he sees the possibility of constructing a linguistics of the *parole organisée* which would be in effect the science of the way language functions. It would attempt to uncover the processes by which *parole* is produced, i.e. to determine how speakers, when they use the resources of the language, come to introduce into it certain peculiar features that bring about modifications. But—and herein lies the originality of Sechehaye's contribution—he considers that these three linguistics fit into a wider framework, that of *parole properly so-called* or the science of natural, pregrammatical expression: the speaker, whose instinct for self-expression impels him to use the resources of *langue* (i.e. the *langue* of the linguistic community he belongs to) exteriorizes these impulses by means of the *parole organisée* in the manifestations of which the evolution of language begins.

We must recall here what we said earlier about diachronic phonology and the way it has successfully overcome the antinomy between synchrony and diachrony.[105] This way of looking at things can be applied to all elements of language. Saussure—in particular when he compared language with chess—had insisted that any change, even an isolated one, has repercussions on the system as a whole,[106] as the equilibrium of the elements of a structure depends on their interdependence and a change effected in any one of them alters the relationships between the different parts of the

---

[102] W. von Wartburg, *Einführung in Problematik und Methodik der Sprachwissenschaft*, 2nd ed., 1962, p. 137 (French translation by P. Maillard, *Problèmes et méthodes de la linguistique*, 2nd ed., Paris, 1963, p. 148). [An English translation by Joyce Reid is shortly to appear in the present series.]

[103] E. Coseriu, *Sincronía, diacronía e historia*, Montevideo, 1958.

[104] A. Sechehaye, 'Les trois linguistiques saussuriennes', in *Vox Romanica*, V, 1940, 1–48.

[105] Pp. 70–72.   [106] Cf. for example *Cours*, pp. 125–126.

system, thereby imperilling the system and causing it to be modified. We are therefore now in a position to conceive of the study of linguistic evolution in the form of *diachronic functionalism*, using the countless and indeed valuable researches of the neogrammarians in such a way as to replace the elements under study into the system they belong to[107] and determine how a modification in the relationships between them leads to a corresponding modification in the structure itself of which they form a part. This is in effect the programme outlined by Benveniste for what he calls diachronic analysis. It consists in 'comparing two successive structures and working out the relationships between them, showing which parts of the previous system were breaking up or were threatened and how the solution reached in later systems was already being prepared', and he makes the pertinent comment: 'In this way the conflict between diachrony and synchrony on which Saussure laid such emphasis is resolved'.[108]

This antinomy however is still held to be valid, at least as a methodological principle, by certain scholars, such as H. Frei, who makes subtle use of the 'semantic square'[109] to account for apparently aberrant changes of meaning,[110] and S. Ullmann, who still regards the contrast between the synchronic and diachronic points of view as obvious and considers that in semantics two complementary subdivisions, the descriptive and the historical,[111] are to be taken into account, stating however that he does so for purely methodological reasons and recognizing that 'there are cases where a combination of the two methods is more fruitful than their strict separation'.[112]

---

[107] See for examples our remarks on phonology, p. 70.

[108] E. Benveniste, 'Tendances récentes' (v. sup., p. 84, n.81), pp. 136–137.

[109] Based on Saussure's 'linguistic square'; v. sup., p. 57 and n. 31.

[110] For example, he accounts for the relationship between the Vedic verbs *pā-* 'to drink' and *utpā* 'to be proud, to rebel' by postulating an earlier meaning of *pā-*, namely 'to flow', and supposing that the verb later became specialized in the meaning of 'to drink':

| *pā-* | *'to flow' | *ud+pā-* | 'to overflow, swell up' |
| *pā-* | 'to drink' | *utpā-* | 'to be proud' |

H. Frei, 'Carrés sémantiques', in *Cahiers Ferdinand de Saussure*, XVI, 1959, 3–22.

[111] S. Ullmann, *The Principles of Semantics*, 2nd ed., Oxford, 1958 (see esp. pp. 139–152).

[112] *Précis de sémantique française*, 2nd ed., Berne, 1959, esp. pp. 38–41.—We shall return later (pp. 136–138) to the problem of synchrony and diachrony in semantics.

Psychological linguistics. The whole of linguistics could of course be included under this heading, for every linguist and every school of thought, even the most positivist, has been concerned at the outset with the fundamental problem of the relationship between language and thought, between sign and concept. Ever since Antiquity, everything has turned on these relationships and Humboldt brought the question once more to the fore in the early days of modern linguistic thinking, and Saussure was to proclaim that 'considered in itself, thought is like a nebula in which there are not necessarily any clear divisions'.[113]

However, the label of psychological linguistics is usually reserved for a school that numbered amongst its promoters at the turn of the century the Danish linguist Otto Jespersen, and found its most complete expression in J. van Ginneken's *Principes de linguistique psychologique* (1907). Thrusting history rather into the background and using with remarkable erudition the data provided by a great number of languages, van Ginneken tries to study the psychic behaviour of the speaker from within and to see how language reacts to the make-up of his own personality. The influence of W. Wundt's *Völkerpsychologie* (Wundt was the founder of experimental psychology), the first part of which had recently been published (1900), can clearly be seen here. A number of studies were to be devoted to the relationship between thought and language, two of the most important being H. Delacroix's *Le langage et la pensée*, 1924, on the psychological plane and F. Brunot's *La pensée et la langue*, 1922, on the linguistic plane with particular reference to French. Since then, there has been an increasing number of studies in this field and it is characteristic that the *Journal de psychologie normale et pathologique* has on several occasions devoted whole issues to problems of linguistics. The fundamental problem of the way a child acquires language has been carefully studied by such linguists as Jespersen, who devoted a large part of his book *Language* to it,[114] Antoine Grégoire, whose work we have already referred to,[115] and R. Jakobson.[116]

So, as the reader can see for himself, the psychological point of view is everywhere present, explicitly or implicitly, in linguistic

---

[113] *Cours*, p. 155.
[114] London, 1922; 11th impression, 1959.
[115] P. 36.
[116] Roman Jakobson, *Kindersprache, Aphasie und allgemeine Lautgesetze*, Uppsala, 1941.

research from whatever standpoint it is carried out, even—as for example in the case of the Bloomfieldians—when psychology is expressly left out of consideration. The very nature of language means that it cannot be otherwise. The actual elaboration and exploitation of the psychological data relating to language form an important chapter of a science that it is not within our competence to treat at any length. It may be pointed out however that work along these lines has given rise to 'psycholinguistics' which, combining the methods of psychology and of linguists, claims to occupy an intermediate position between these two sciences.[117]

The sociological school. That language is a social fact (we speak because we live in society) may well appear to be a truism that needs no lengthy justification. All those who are in any way concerned with the study of social groups know that a knowledge of language is fundamental to their research and one of the essential means for carrying out their task and for acquiring further data and for checking their results. It would seem that linguists, for whom language is not an intermediary but the very object of their study, should readily endorse the view that language is a social fact. But in reality, if the sociological character of language has never been denied, the ways in which this has influenced the elaboration of linguistic doctrines have been many and varied. It is particularly in France that a theory based on the common-sense observation of the social character of language has emerged. It is indeed a somewhat hazy theory, far removed from any dogmatic approach,[118] but one that, based as it is on the study of sociological relationships (which form the essence of linguistic communities), is stimulated and actualized by contact with social realities. The sociological spirit animating the leaders of the French school is well shown in Joseph Vendryes' excellent book, *Le langage*.[119]

[117] Cf. G. A. Miller, *Language and Communication*, New York, 1951; S. Saporta and J. R. Bastian (ed.), *Psycholinguistics: a book of readings*, New York, 1961; C. E. Osgood, 'Language Universals and Psycholinguistics', in J. H. Greenberg, *Universals of Language*, Cambridge, Mass., 1963; R. Titone, *La psicolinguistica oggi*, Zurich, 1964 (this book provides a clear picture of trends in research and an extensive bibliography).

[118] In the preface to Marcel Cohen's *Cinquante années de recherches linguistiques, ethnologiques, sociologiques, critiques et pédagogiques*, Paris, 1955, J. Vendryes wrote: 'Though there is no French school of linguistics, claiming any exclusive privilege, there does exist amongst Meillet's pupils a mutual feeling of comprehension and friendly collaboration in applying to linguistics the rules of enlightened reason'.

[119] Finished in 1914 but not published till 1920.

Of course, since the time of Jean-Jacques Rousseau and his view, formed long before sociology came into being, of the 'general will', an appeal to the 'social consciousness' has been no novelty in scientific thinking[120] but it is to the credit of the French linguists that, around the postulate that 'language is first and foremost a social fact',[121] they were able to draw up the principles that seemed to account for the facts of language. On the historical plane in particular they have sought to elucidate the ways in which a given language has evolved by considering them as reflections of the changes that have taken place in the human society whose means of expression it is.

As linguistic activity is a function of the imitative instinct—an instinct that sociologists agree in considering to be one of the most deeply engrained in the heredity of social beings—it follows that one imitates those whom one admires and loves because one wants to be like them. The child learns to speak by trying to reproduce the language of his parents and those around him. He is impelled to do this by the imitative instinct and also by the instinct of attraction: the need to make himself understood, the need to feel himself more closely integrated into the social group he belongs to. Adults may modify their language to bring it closer to that of people they consider as models. As a general principle, we can say that speakers imitate those who have a certain prestige, that is, those who arouse in them the propensity to imitate them.[122] Whether this imitation

---

[120] It is worth recalling what Rousseau wrote to Du Peyron: 'Whether or not an expression is "good French" or "good usage" is not the point; one speaks or writes only in order to make oneself understood; provided one is intelligible, one achieves one's aim; when one is clear in addition, one achieves it even better. Therefore, speak so as to be clear to anyone who understands French, that is the rule and you can be quite sure that, even if you perpetrate five hundred barbarisms, you will not have written any the worse on that account. I will go further and maintain that it is sometimes necessary to commit mistakes of grammar in order to be absolutely clear; that, and not all the purists' pedantries, is what constitutes the true art of good writing' (*Correspondance générale*, XIII, 220–221). Cf. G. Redard, 'Langue française et patois', in *IVe Cahier de l'Institut neuchâtelois*, 1954, p. 14.

[121] The quotation is from Meillet's inaugural lecture at the Collège de France, delivered on 17th Feb., 1906, and entitled *L'État actuel des études de linguistique générale*—but 'general linguistics' here does not mean the same thing as today; at that time it referred to comparative and historical grammar. The lecture was reprinted in *Linguistique historique et linguistique générale*, I, Paris, 1921, pp. 1–18, see esp. p. 16. On p. 18 we read: 'The aim of this course of lectures therefore will be to investigate to what extent relationships between linguistic development and other social facts can be established at the present time'.

[122] Cf. E. Dupréel, *Sociologie générale*, Paris, 1948, pp. 59–68, 286–287.

is conscious or unconscious is immaterial, it provides the clue to many of the problems presented by linguistic evolution.

Who are these 'leaders' whose prestige sways a whole population in its way of speaking, its pronunciation, the choice of words, even mannerisms and wrong usages? They are first and foremost the ruling classes who play a considerable role in any organized society. In France, under the Ancien Régime, the court and the salons dictated linguistic as well as social manners and only the speech of this minority was held to be correct. The Revolution brought to power a social class whose speech, hitherto considered vulgar and incorrect, soon came to share in the prestige conferred on this class by its newly acquired political responsibilities. Thus it was that pronunciations that are attested since the sixteenth century but that had hitherto been considered vulgar (such as the pronunciation [rwa] *roi* instead of [rwɛ] or [batajɔ̃] *bataillon* instead of the earlier [bataʎɔ̃] with a palatal *l*) were immediately accepted and rapidly passed into common use.

The prestige of cultural and artistic groups is no less influential. Circles of writers, especially when they are grouped in academies supported by the state, have an appreciable moderating and conservative effect on the official language that is held up as a model for the whole of the linguistic community. And the far reaching influence of the school-master is well known: Romance linguists quote the example of Latin final -*s* which was pronounced only lightly, perhaps even fleetingly, and so has left no trace in Italian (Latin *murus*: Italian *muro*), whereas in Gaul and the Iberian peninsula where Latin was at first an imported language that was taught to the natives, the -*s* was preserved or perhaps restored under the influence (reinforced perhaps by native speech habits) of the schools (e.g. Old French nominative *murs* < *murus*, oblique *mur* < *murum*). In our own day, the action of schools has been considerably strengthened by the introduction of compulsory education, and ease of communications has multiplied contacts. And there is no need to stress the importance of radio and television in contemporary civilization.

The method adopted by the supporters of the sociological school consists therefore in explaining linguistic data by extralinguistic factors, and it is clear that the solution to the problem depends on the choice made by the linguist amongst the factors that could be operative. The result will depend on how strongly he considers one or other factor to be preponderant or decisive. Indeed, as in all the human sciences, the history of linguistic thinking is merely the history of the efforts made to classify the data. We are all the time brought back to the question, that we have already had occasion to refer to,[123] of the choice and evaluation of criteria.

From the early years of this century, which also mark the beginnings of its outstanding period and its prestige, the French school of linguistics has borne the unquestionable stamp of the sociological spirit ('the social sciences are now in the process of being constituted, and linguistics must take amongst them the place assigned to it by its very nature')[124] and Meillet did not hesitate to pay renewed tribute to the teaching of a scholar such as Durkheim.[125]

'A language', he said, 'is a highly organized system of means of expression common to a body of speakers. The system does not exist apart from the individuals who speak (or write) the language. It nevertheless exists independently of each one of them, for it imposes itself on them. Its reality is that of a social institution, immanent in individuals, but at the same time independent of each one of them.'[126] The danger clearly is that the myth may be revived of language considered as an independent, supra-individual entity— not a natural organism this time but a social one, situated in the 'collective consciousness' (the expression is Durkheim's and can even be considered as the keystone of his theories)[127] of the speakers. This danger was to increase with the widespread acceptance of

---

[123] V. sup., p. 74.

[124] Meillet, in his 1906 lecture at the Collège de France (v. sup., p. 94, n. 121) (=Linguistique historique et linguistique générale, I, p. 18). Thirty years later Vendryes was still asserting the pre-eminently social nature of language in the chapter entitled 'La linguistique' that he contributed to the collective work Les sciences sociales en France: Enseignement et Recherches, Paris, 1937, pp. 100–117.

[125] In the introductory lecture to his course on 'General principles of the evolution of language', 1901 (Revue de l'Université de Bruxelles, VII, 1901–1902, 257–280), P. de Reul spoke of the recourse to social factors to explain linguistic facts as something new and referred to the 'sociological point of view in the history of language' (this indeed was the title of his lecture) as being 'an aspect of language that has not received sufficient attention'; cf. É. Buyssens, "Du point de vue sociologique en linguistique' in Notes et conférences, V, Brussels, 1947, 29–64.

[126] Meillet in an article, 'Le développement des langues', that appeared in 1929 in the volume Continu et discontinu and was reproduced in Linguistique historique et linguistique générale, II, Paris, 1936, p. 72.

[127] Cf. for example W. Doroszewski, 'Quelques remarques sur les rapports de la sociologie et de la linguistique: Durkheim et F. de Saussure', in Journal de Psychologie, XXX, 1933, 82–91.

Saussure's distinction between *langue* and *parole* which was to strengthen markedly the theories of the sociological school. This distinction laid emphasis on *langue* which is 'social in essence and independent of the individual'[128] and is conceived of as a system of signs serving as a means of communication for the members of a given linguistic community ('It is the whole set of linguistic habits that enable an individual to understand and to be understood'),[129] whilst *parole* is an individual act, the use that each person makes of the system (*langue*) of the linguistic community he belongs to in order to understand and be understood.

It will be noted, however, that as a direct result of the emphasis he laid on the social factor, Meillet, a fervent follower of Saussure, was one of the first to reproach Saussurian linguistics with being too abstract. Time and again[130] he drew attention to the human reality surrounding language: as something created by man, language shares all the conditions and vicissitudes of human existence. Everything in language, said Vendryes,[131] 'is dominated by social conditions, for the phenomenon "language" is the social phenomenon *par excellence*, and it is the fact that it is a social phenomenon that provides the study of language with a general method of research and explanation'. This concern to view linguistics, which he termed 'the first-born of the human sciences', from the sociological point of view, and to give it at the same time a Marxist orientation[132] pervades the many important and varied publications of another of Meillet's pupils, Marcel Cohen.[133]

Mention must be made too of the work of Georges Dumézil. As a linguist he is concerned, like the members of the Italian school with whom he has much in common,[134] to combine the comparative method with the data provided by the history of civilizations, seeking to uncover the concepts underlying words and structures, to analyse beliefs, to trace the limits of social and religious configurations. He has succeeded in this way in rehabilitating 'comparative

---

[128] *Cours*, p. 37.
[129] *Cours*, p. 112.
[130] Cf. the two volumes of collected articles, *Linguistique historique et linguistique générale*, Paris, I, 1921 (reprinted 1948), II, 1936.
[131] *Bulletin de la Société de Linguistique de Paris*, XLVII, fasc. 2, 1951, p. 49.
[132] V. inf., p. 119.
[133] See in particular his book *Pour une sociologie du langage*, Paris, 1956.
[134] V. inf., p. 106.

mythology', that the primitivist and *a priori* conceptions of Max Müller had brought to grief.[135]

Others, going beyond the historical data, have taken up again the old problem of the origin of language,[136] but this time on more modest and at the same time sounder and scientifically acceptable foundations, studying on the one hand the contribution that can be made by prehistory to the elucidation of problems of language[137] and on the other the relationship of *homo sapiens* to his environment and his group.[138] The fact that a journal has recently been founded with a linguist, a geographer and an ethnologist[139] on its editorial board augurs well for the future.

The sociological point of view has spread far beyond France. It was for example one of the sources of the work of L. Bloomfield whose book *Language* (1933)[140] marked an epoch in the United States where it enjoys immense prestige. Yet Bloomfield could not but offend a number of his compatriots by defending a distinctly materialist theory (leaving awareness, which is not susceptible to scientific investigation, out of account, he explains the mechanism of communication as a succession of stimuli and responses).[141] On the other hand, E. Sapir, though a determined adversary of Bloomfield's materialist views,[142] was nevertheless also influenced by sociological theories, in that in his view a language constituted for its speakers a powerful symbol of kinship.

[135] The reader who wants a guide to the extensive work of G. Dumézil will find a résumé of his views in his volume *L'Idéologie tripartie des Indo-Européens*, Brussels, 1958; he abstracts from the structure of the ancient Indo-European societies what seems to him to be their essential awareness of a tripartite division of the world: sovereignty (the way the world is governed), might (physical strength) and fecundity, corresponding to the three social classes of priests, warriors and tillers of the soil, organized in a system that operates in space, in time and in human activity.

[136] V. sup., pp. 24–26.

[137] Cf. A. Tovar, 'Linguistics and Prehistory' in *Word*, X, 1954, 333–350.

[138] Cf. H. Hoijer, 'Anthropological Linguistics', in *Trends in European and American Linguistics, 1930–1960* (v. sup., p. vii), pp. 110–127.

[139] The reference is to the journal *L'Homme*, founded in 1961 and edited by É. Benveniste, P. Gourou and C. Levi-Strauss.—The *International Anthropological and Linguistic Review*, that started in 1953, in spite of its title devotes only little space to linguistics and what it does publish in this field is not always very reliable.

[140] *Language* is in fact a second and considerably recast version of his book *An Introduction to the Study of Language*, which appeared in 1914.

[141] Cf. C. C. Fries, 'The Bloomfield "School"', in *Trends in European and American Linguistics, 1930–1960* (v. sup., p. vii), pp. 196–224.—Cf. sup., pp. 83–84 et inf., p. 116.

[142] V. inf., pp. 116–117.

Many linguists, among them the Norwegian Alf Sommerfelt, also attempted—not without encountering great difficulties that were sometimes due to the inadequacy of the available data—to relate the linguistic structure of a given dialect to the social organization of the community whose means of expression it is. It is also of interest to recall the very different and thoroughly pragmatic way in which the linguist's social mission is envisaged by the British phonetician Daniel Jones: 'In contrast with workers in some other scientific fields, they [i.e. linguists] can keep in mind throughout their investigations a definite humanistic object towards which they can direct their attention, namely the improvement of the means of oral and written communication between man and man. The findings of phonetic science give people skill in communicating effectively with each other.'[143]

In a similar vein, we may recall the efforts, now apparently abandoned,[144] of the I.A.L.A. (International Auxiliary Language Association) to create an 'international auxiliary language' which they thought of as an artificial language that could be superimposed on—or even, according to the most optimistic views, replace—national languages. A noble idea, no doubt, and one that resulted in a number of schemes (the best known being Esperanto) but which is quite illusory, at least insofar as the aim was to create anything more than a system of symbols that, in the same way as mathematical formulae, could serve, if only within necessarily narrow limits, as a means of communication in the field of one or other of the sciences. Apart from this limited application, the unity of any such artificial language would soon be threatened and destroyed by the fundamental structural differences amongst the mother tongues of those who learned it and above all by the complete absence of any cultural background that could bolster it up.[145]

The following examination of the various ways in which linguistic research has been coloured by taking into account the individual factor will provide a further opportunity for discussing social theories.[146]

[143] *The Phoneme*, Cambridge, 1950, p. 218.
[144] Cf. André Martinet, in *Bulletin de la Société de Linguistique de Paris*, LVII, 2, 1962, 30–34.
[145] The first full discussion of this problem of interlinguistics took place at the 1948 Paris Congress: see *Actes du Sixième Congrès International des Linguistes*, Paris, 1949, pp. 93–112, 409–416, 585–600.
[146] Pp. 106–108.

The individualist theses. In Vol. XXX of the Acts of the Accademia Pontaniana of Naples, Croce published in 1900 three papers he had read at the February, March and April meetings of the Academy. These are his *Tesi fondamentali di un'Estetica come scienza dell'espressione e linguistica generale*. Moved by the desire to define the difference between history and art, he laid down in this work the foundations of a doctrine that proclaimed the specificity of art and carried the study of language over into the realm of aesthetics. Two years later, under the title *Estetica come scienza dell'espressione e linguistica generale*, Croce reissued the same text followed by a historical part, *Storia dell'Estetica*, a few chapters of which had been published the previous year in the Neapolitan journal, *Flegrea*. This was the origin of the first of the four great volumes (*Aesthetics—Logic—Philosophy of the Practical—Historiography*) that were later issued under the collective title of *Philosophy of the Spirit*. The *Aesthetics* stands out among the many writings of the great Italian philosopher; this 'arid and abstruse' work which, according to his own testimony, cost him much toil, remorse and revision, was considered by its author as a programme, as the draft of another work still be to written for, he says, he realized when going through the proofs that 'this book in which I thought I had emptied my brain of all the philosophy that had accumulated in it had instead filled it with new philosophy'.[147]

'General linguistics': the expression appears in the full title of the volume devoted to aesthetics. The unsuspecting student opening Croce's book with the purpose of completing his knowledge of linguistics or deepening the ideas he had picked up at his lectures would certainly be disappointed, or at any rate rather put out, for he would find in it nothing of the traditional framework of general linguistics, nothing even recalling it very precisely except perhaps a fierce criticism of the manuals in use at the beginning of the century—those in the Brugmann tradition—in which 'one generally finds a bit of everything: from a description of the speech organs and the artificial machines capable of imitating it (gramophones) to summaries of the most important achievements in the Indo-European, Semitic, Coptic, Chinese or some other philological field, from philosophical generalities on the origin or nature of language to advice on format, calligraphy and how to classify one's

[147] *Contributo alla Critica di me stesso*, Bari, 1926, pp. 39 and 41.

index cards for purposes of philological investigations'.[148] At the time this was a most disrespectful criticism.

In fact, after expressing his views on language in the *Estetica*, Croce rarely returned to the subject, and then only to restate the same views, to clarify certain points, or to rectify certain misconceptions. Furthermore, he never took any interest in the technical aspects of linguistic research. And yet his ideas had far-reaching repercussions on the nature and direction of the work of two particularly active and original schools of linguistics: the members of the idealist school and the adherents of neolinguistics (*la neolinguistica*) could justly claim to be his followers, associating with his name that of Vico whose work, that was published some 175 years before but had long remained unrecognized (except possibly in Italy at the time of the *Risorgimento*), only became influential and appreciated as a result of Croce's penetrating criticism and studies.

We have already outlined the underlying principles of the *Scienza nuova*.[149] It will easily be understood how Croce could turn it to account and base himself on his distinguished predecessor when constructing his philosophy of the spirit and his theory of expression. For the problem of expression is in fact at the heart of Croce's aesthetic—and linguistic—preoccupations. He identifies intuition and expression, intuitive knowledge is expressive knowledge and all intuition is at the same time expression. Thought cannot exist apart from expression; it is false to believe that language is an instrument forged by man for the purpose of communicating with his fellows: language, which is wholly intuitive by nature, arises spontaneously with the mental picture it expresses, for, if man does not speak, he does not think. On the question of the origin of language, Croce follows Vico in declaring that language was born as poetry and afterwards took on the functions of a sign.[150]

Croce's teaching takes the study of concrete linguistic data out of the descriptive field of normative grammars and out of the elaborate theorizing of the comparatists and places it in the sphere of aesthetics. Indeed in his view grammar is merely an informative discipline[151]

---

[148] B. Croce, *Estetica*, quarta edizione riveduta, Bari, 1912, p. 174.

[149] V. sup., pp. 8–9.

[150] Cf. J. Lameere, *L'Esthétique de Benedetto Croce*, Paris, 1936, esp pp. 117–137.

[151] Croce, recalling Voltaire's *tant pis pour la grammaire*, even considers a 'normative grammar' as an impossibility: language is neither an arbitrary nor a voluntary fact and the art of writing (Croce is thinking especially of the literary language) is acquired not by observing rules but by reading and by example.

H

or, to put it differently, a paedagogical expedient, a system of mnemonics that is useful and necessary in practice, but is not in any sense of the word a science. The comparative and historical study of grammar forms part of the history of languages in their living reality, i.e. principally the history of literary works, and here we see the deliberate confusion between the study of language and literary criticism. Furthermore, linguistic signs have meaning only if they are considered to be inextricably bound up with the expressive impulse that for a moment lives, then dies and is never repeated in exactly identical fashion. For language is expression. Indeed, a series of sounds that expresses nothing is not language: language is articulate sound organized for purposes of expression. And Croce concludes that aesthetics and linguistics are not two distinct sciences but one and the same, and adds that languages do not exist apart from actual spoken or written statements made by certain peoples at given periods of time, in other words they do not exist apart from the works of art in which they have concrete existence.

For years, either out of scorn or out of ignorance, linguists, or at any rate the great majority of them, made no response whatsoever to this doctrine. It is true that it came at a time when the rigid principles of the neogrammarians went almost unchallenged. We have already mentioned[152] how the neogrammarians, reacting against the methodological laxity and the rather fanciful enthusiasm of the early comparatists, had perfected a strict method and proclaimed the doctrine of the infallibility and blind, mechanical working of the sound laws. Their naïve confidence in the perfection of the tool they had forged led them to despise the heretical theses defended by the Italian thinker, so that he is nowhere mentioned or even alluded to in Meillet's celebrated *Introduction* or any of the other manuals of the neogrammarian school. And when the *Cours de linguistique générale* appeared, it was immediately obvious that there was a fundamental incompatibility between Croce's conception of spontaneous, continuous creation and Saussure's views on the constraints imposed by society (the choice of signs is not free).

In contrast to the almost unanimous lack of understanding of Croce's views, one linguist took up the cudgels on their behalf from the outset and made an enthusiastic attempt to apply them to the practical, concrete study of linguistic data. This was Karl

[152] Pp. 30–32.

Vossler, a Romance philologist from Munich, who remained on terms of unwavering friendship with Croce for a period of fifty years during which they shared the same intellectual ideals, in spite of very different political fortunes.[153] Vossler's attempt to transpose the philosophical element—the only one Croce had been concerned with—on to the purely linguistic plane was not without its problems. He did indeed proclaim, like Croce, that linguistics is really aesthetics and that stylistics—the study of the means of expression—must be placed at the very centre of linguistics, but from his very earliest works (cf. his characteristically entitled *Positivismus und Idealismus in der Sprachwissenschaft*, 1904) he finds himself forced, 'provisionally' and empirically at any rate, to preserve the traditional divisions of the study of language and break out of the narrow framework of the equation 'linguistics — aesthetics' by moving on from the study of stylistics and syntax to that of morphology and phonetics. He maintains that all linguistic evolution is, in the last analysis, a matter of taste, that is, of the speaker's aesthetic sense, and that all linguistic expression is an individual creation, but in order to explain why these countless individual acts of initiative do not lead to anarchy he is obliged to invoke a certain passivity of the linguistic system that limits its possibilities for creative invention. Linguistic innovations are to be envisaged from two different points of view: when an innovation is introduced into language, there is 'absolute progress' the study of which comes within the scope of aesthetics; when an innovation spreads, there is 'relative progress' for this is not creation but extension and must be studied both from the aesthetic point of view and from that of traditional historical grammar.

Furthermore, Vossler and his followers in the idealist school[154] (amongst the most active of them were Eugen Lerch and Leo Spitzer) strenuously opposed—and herein perhaps lies the most fruitful part of their work—the concluding statement of the *Cours* that 'the one and only true object of linguistics is language envisaged in and for itself'. No, replies Vossler, the study of a language is inseparable from that of the corresponding culture; even historical grammar, with all its technical apparatus, forms part of *Kultur-*

153 The *Carteggio Croce-Vossler*, published at Bari in 1951 and including all the important letters exchanged between the two friends from Nov. 1899 to the end of 1948, a few months before Vossler's death on 18th May, 1949, is a valuable source of information on the intellectual movement during the first half of the twentieth century, but it also has a moving human value.
154 Cf. for example R. A. Hall, *Idealism in Romance Linguistics*, Ithaca, 1963.

geschichte, since it is one of the criteria by which the civilization of a people may be understood and appreciated; the history of a language embraces in reality all aspects of spiritual and intellectual life. And it is not difficult to understand why the members of the idealist school devoted far greater attention to literary languages than to popular forms of speech, so that Schuchardt—who had a certain sympathy with the idealist school—remarked that Vossler was concerned with *homo sapientissimus* whereas he himself was interested in *homo sapiens* who was not far removed from *homo alalus*.[155]

The Italian G. Bertoni whose name has often been associated with that of Vossler—who, however, publicly disagreed with him more than once—also follows Croce when he maintains that the only linguistic reality is individual language and that there is no thought without expression (the expression is not the 'garment' but the 'body itself' of thought), but his efforts to combine spirit (aesthetic expression) and nature (the datum), in other words the theses of the idealists and the methods of positivist naturalism, produced a synthesis that he himself considered eclectic but which in fact seems contradictory, so that it has been said that, in the field of research inspired by Croce's aesthetics, Bertoni was the symbol of the valiant fighter on whom fortune has not smiled.[156] Likewise, his distinction between *linguaggio* and *lingua*, the first being the (individual) activity of the spirit, the second the (collective) product of this activity ('Il linguaggio è l'anima della lingua') was not admitted by Croce who saw in it a blend of his own teaching and the 'anaesthetic and antiaesthetic' actualism of Gentile.

On the other hand, another and very fruitful trend deriving from Croce developed in Italy. This was Matteo Bartoli's *neolinguistica*. The manifesto of the new school was Bartoli's *Introduzione alla neolinguistica*, 1925, but he had already set out the principles of it in 1910[157] and the first seeds had been sown in his mind as early as 1902

---

[155] Hugo Schuchardt (1842–1927), another who took an individual line at the time of the neogrammarians, advocated, in opposition to the dogma of historical relationship, his view of 'linguistic affinity' (cf. inf., p. 122), representing linguistic evolution as the resultant of two forces: centrifugal individualism and (to employ a Saussurian term before Saussure) social constraint, attempting in this way to harmonize positivist data with an idealist interpretation: 'Born of necessity, language reaches its highest point in art': *Schuchardt-Brevier* (cf. sup., p. 51, n. 7), p. 265.

[156] G. Devoto, in *Cinquant'anni di vita intellettuale italiana*, Vol. I, Naples, 1950, p. 375.

[157] In his study *Alle fonti del neolatino*; cf. G. Bonfante, 'The neolinguistic position', in *Language*, XXIII, 1947, 364.

when he read the *Estetica*.[158] Indeed Bartoli, who had already made a name for himself with solid, well-documented studies on Vulgar Latin and the Romance dialects, was to follow the impetus he had received from Croce far less blindly than Vossler, whom he does not hestitate to accuse of having no sense of linguistic realities, but also far more fruitfully than Bertoni who, although he joined with Bartoli in publishing the *Breviario di neolinguistica* in 1928, had been led astray, as we have seen, along the path of rather muddled specutions.

What Bartoli owed above all to Croce was complete independence in face of the doctrinaire systematizing of the neogrammarians and a reasoned dislike of materialist explanations of the processes of evolution. He combats the idea that the 'sound-laws', on which the neogrammarians placed such importance, work blindly like an irresistible physiological force. He refuses to allow the traditional division between 'grammar' and 'vocabulary' anything more than a purely practical interest and maintains that this division does not call for two different methods of interpretation. He is convinced that the spread of linguistic innovations, whether lexical or grammatical (phonetic, morphological, syntactical), operates in the same way and that, to account for them, one must take into account imitation, the prestige of the models as well as the more or less aesthetic creative 'fancy' of the speakers. Here we find once more the equations that Croce was so fond of: fancy=poetry, poetry=language, *ergo* language=fancy.

In short, Bartoli proclaims that linguistics must be a human science, embracing language in its entirety, relating it to other creations of the mind (such as literature, the arts and so on) and looking upon it as one facet of the history of mankind.

It must be emphasized that, as Bartoli and the neolinguists readily acknowledged, another dominating influence, parallel to that of Croce, also marked the development of the principles and methods of the school (for neolinguistics appears as something of an eclecticism), and this was linguistic geography, that had just been made into an independent discipline by Gilliéron. Taking over into the field of the ancient Indo-European languages methods worked out

[158] Cf. the anecdote related by Croce (*Quaderni della Critica*, V, No. 15, Nov. 1949, 119–120) according to which Bartoli showed his students the *Estetica* that he had just read and told them, as if completely overwhelmed: 'Giovani miei, abbiamo sbagliato, dobbiamo rifarci da capo: questo libro lo prova'.

and tested in the field of living dialects made it possible to draw up principles for classifying the Indo-European dialects and determining the relationships between them. Thus it was that Indo-European dialectology, to which we shall return later,[159] came into being.

Leaving aside various questions of technical detail, we shall try and characterize neolinguistics in its broadest sense and so determine to what extent Croce's ideas have influenced the development and progress of the science of language. In fact, the work of the neolinguists, paralleled by that of scholars taking a different approach, contributed to a not inconsiderable extent in forming a number of the conceptions and ways of looking at our discipline that are now part of the common heritage of all linguists.

Not the least of the merits of neolinguistics was its declared intention of restoring to linguistics its status as a human science. The time has gone when a course in comparative grammar could be restricted to a dry statement of correspondences presented with a profusion of asterisks. This rigid schematization—very useful for teaching purposes!—must make way for a more subtle, more flexible but also more complex picture that is more in keeping with the understanding of human realities with which problems of language should be studied.

Another feature of Italian linguistics is the effort made by its leading figures to provide linguistics with what G. Devoto—who has recently given a new and masterly illustration of the method in his *Origini Indeuropee*[160]—calls a horizontal organization by collaborating closely in the study of each and every problem with parallel sciences such as history, law and archaeology. For the Saussurian notion of *system*, Devoto and Nencioni substitute that of *institution*, which takes account of the twofold aspect, social and individual, of linguistic data.[161]

The concern to take account of the aesthetic factor and the attention paid to individual values remain a dominating feature of the research carried on by our Italian colleagues. We can therefore understand why neolinguists react so strongly against the dogmatism of the neogrammarians, stressing the importance of the human value of language and the fact that it is a continuous creation, or rather,

---

[159] Pp. 111–116.   [160] Florence, 1962.
[161] Cf. for example G. Devoto, *I Fondamenti della storia linguistica*, Florence, 1951, G. Nencioni, *Idealismo e realismo nella scienza del linguaggio*, Florence, 1946.

since it is imitation, a re-creation. Now imitation is never a mechanically exact reproduction: there is therefore a constant elaboration
of data giving rise to new creations the success of which depends on
various factors such as the prestige of those imitated or their creative
power, one important factor being the aesthetic value of the innovation. The acceptance of a linguistic innovation by the speakers of the
language often presupposes a choice, i.e. an aesthetic judgment.
Contrary to the view of the neogrammarians that the forces governing the evolution of language operate on it irresistibly and as it were
mechanically and unbeknown to the speakers, the neolinguists hold
that the individual element is primordial and that the conscious action
of artists, writers and poets plays a considerable part in linguistic
phenomena in general.

In short, then, the neolinguists achieved a felicitous synthesis
by combining the strictest type of comparative grammar and the
classic methods of traditional linguistics with a respect for the
creative spirit and aesthetic sense of the human personality. To take
the problem of linguistic innovations and the way they spread: this
is a case where the role of *parole*, an individual act, seems to be
preponderant. The linguists of the sociological school, in accordance
with Saussure's teaching ('of all social institutions, language is the
one that offers least scope for initiative'),[162] tried to interpret this
role of the individual in a social sense. J. Vendryes, for example,
whilst not denying the role of the individual, declared in 1921 that
'it cannot be admitted without some restriction' and opposed the
view that an innovation is to be understood as 'an individual fact
generalized by imitation'. He continued: 'It is certain that any linguistic change results solely from the use that an individual makes of
the language. But what other than a social cause can introduce into
langue the change thus created in *parole*? It may well be admitted
that a new usage always begins with a series of individual acts, provided one recognizes at the same time that these individual acts
create a new usage solely because they correspond to a collective
tendency. Facts belonging to *parole* are no more than particular
and occasional ways in which individuals use the established system.
But it is only by virtue of a tacit agreement amongst all the speakers
of the language that they result in anything general and permanent.
We must therefore speak not of individual innovations that have

[162] *Cours*, pp. 107-108.

been generalized but rather of general innovations that manifest themselves in isolated individuals.'[163] In 1937, in an important contribution in which he brought out the eminently social value of language,[164] the same author, after saying that 'the history of any language is a succession of accidents, but of collective accidents', was nevertheless prompted to attribute a certain influence to 'individual accidents' so long as these were sanctioned by the community; and he added: 'The rise of Victor Hugo or Voltaire is only one of the countless accidents that come about in the life of a language and to which each speaker of the language makes his own contribution. Great writers certainly have a preponderant role. The part played by each individual depends on his personal authority, on the prestige he enjoys, on the influence he exerts in the environment in which he lives.'

We have quoted these passages because they seem to typify the author's deliberate attempt to explain linguistic facts as being *a priori* social facts. The neolinguists readily acknowledged the inventive capacity of the individual or rather of certain individuals, since, when they compare the spread of linguistic innovations with the spread of literature, the arts or, say, women's fashions, they emphasize that the personality of the innovator is preponderant and they credit the aesthetic factor with an importance that their predecessors were very far from admitting. For the blind, mechanical working of the forces of evolution corresponding to a 'collective tendency', they substitute the reasoned influx of a conscious force. For those linguists who adopted Croce's ideas, this was yet another reason for according preferential treatment to the study of literary works which reflect the individual efforts of artists and writers. As Devoto put it, literary languages are not *anormalità* but are just as natural as any other form of language.

Is there any need to add that the formulation and proclamation of Croce's linguistic principles are in line with the intellectual and cultural tradition of Italy? And it is surely not a matter of chance that it was in Italy and Germany that the individualist theories on language were the most successfully defended and developed. For, contrary to what has usually been the case elsewhere—and in particular in France where political unification preceded and in large

---

[163] 'Le caractère social du langage et la doctrine de F. de Saussure', in *Journal de Psychologie*, XVIII, 1921, 622–623 (=*Choix d'études linguistiques et celtiques*, p. 23).
[164] Viz., his study *La linguistique* referred to above, p. 96, n. 124.

measure imposed linguistic unification (one thinks for example of the *Ordonnance de Villers-Cotterets* [1539] and the centralization of the French state, under every regime, from the seventeenth century onwards)—in Italy and Germany the unity of the language or, more exactly, the choice of one form of language rather than another as the prevalent form preceded or even prepared the way for political unity. One has only to consider that it was owing to Dante and his phenomenal *Divine Comedy* that the Tuscan dialect came to be the model for Italian which later became the official language of the whole peninsula, or that it was the complex Middle High German norm used by Luther in his translation of the Bible that was later adopted as a model in all the German-speaking countries.

And this also explains the particular position of Saussure's work in Italy. We have already mentioned Saussure's outstanding role and the fact that he can be considered the father of modern linguistics and the inspiration behind some of the most active and combative schools of thought. But there is this exception that, in spite of its considerable prestige that has shown itself in the constant flow of work it has inspired, the effect of Saussure's work in Italy has been less profound than in most other countries. A few linguists, it is true, such as G. Devoto or T. Bolelli, can claim to be Saussurians, but in a very independent and 'anticonformist' fashion. It is true also that the teachings of the *Cours* have been expounded and studied in Italy, but rather it would seem for purposes of information than out of acceptance or approbation. Indeed, the neolinguists have taken hardly any part in the great debates of recent years concerning the principles laid down by Saussure (such as the arbitrary nature of the sign, the differential quality of the elements of language, etc.) and very few of them are prepared to engage in the abstract speculations towards which some of the schools deriving from Saussure's teaching are seeking to lead us today. But after all what possible significance can the antinomy *langue/parole*[165] and the importance attached to the system envisaged as being outside of and above individuals have for linguists who are convinced of the importance of the individual factor in facts of language and of the relevance to such facts of the aesthetic sense of the individual speaker? And the other notorious distinction, between synchrony and diachrony, which as we have

---

[165] Bertoni's antinomy *lingua/linguaggio* that we have already referred to (p. 104) had been formulated independently of Saussure's theory and in a different sense.

already seen[166] had been attacked by von Wartburg, met with only a feeble response in Italy. Let us not forget moreover that Croce—in agreement for once with the neogrammarians—always insisted that the true nature of linguistics is to be a historical discipline.

This 'a-Saussurian' attitude has been one of the notable characteristics of the Italian school of linguistics. Only the phenomenal intellect, the spiritual authority and expressive force of Benedetto Croce could have neutralized to some extent the persuasiveness and undeniable intellectual appeal of Ferdinand de Saussure's work. For it was Croce's lot to impart even to linguistics, a field he only touched on without ever going into its technical aspect, an impetus that led to new ways of looking at the facts with the result that, since the beginning of the twentieth century, Italy has occupied a privileged position in the history of research.[167]

In reality, in this debate between the individual and the social factors, it has to be recognized that, once again, each side has sometimes taken up an extreme position whereas an intermediate solution might well be found as in the case of Saussure's antinomies between synchrony and diachrony and between *langue* and *parole*. One might perhaps invoke the idea of progress, not as conceived of—somewhat naïvely—by Jespersen,[168] as the supreme explanation of linguistic evolution, but as representing men's aspiration towards a certain perfection. For is not this obsession with progress a remarkable motivating force in human activity and should one not acknowledge the effort of the poet or prose writer to attain more nearly to the Beautiful through language? Of course, language is the collective and continuous product of all members of a social group. Consciously or otherwise, each of us introduces into it certain innovations but these can only become the rule if they are accepted and adopted by the linguistic community as a whole. To fulfil this condition, not

---

[166] V. sup., pp. 89–90.

[167] It must be pointed out that in recent years increasing attention has been paid in Italy to Saussure's theories, as an interest in structuralism developed; cf. for example L. Heilmann, 'Orientamenti strutturali dell'indagine linguistica', in *Rendiconti dell'-Accademia dei Lincei*, Classe di sc. mor., VII, 10 (1955), 136–156; W. Belardi, *Elementi di fonologia*, Rome, 1959; T. de Mauro, *Storia linguistica dell'Italia unita*, Bari, 1963; G. Lepschy, 'Aspetti teorici di alcuni correnti della glottologia contemporanea', in *Annali della Scuola normale di Pisa*, s. II, Vol. XXX, 1961, 187–267; the following works by A. Pagliaro are particularly instructive in this respect: *Nuovi saggi di critica semantica*, Messina-Florence, 1956; *La parola e l'immagine*, Naples, 1957; *Altri saggi di critica semantica*, Messina-Florence, 1961.

[168] V. sup., pp. 43–44.

only must the innovator have a certain prestige but the change he is proposing must correspond to the feeling of the speakers in general.

This means that the chances that any particular change, whether accidental or deliberate, will succeed are infinitesimal. And it must be stressed that in the work of continual creation that is language, some individuals, artists, play a greater part than others. The writer uses the common language (this is an indispensable condition, for a poet who is not understood by anyone else is not, from the point of view of his artistic production, a social being) but he has greater awareness than others of the resources it offers. He succeeds in creating combinations of sounds, forms or meanings that make an aesthetic impression on the hearer or reader and awaken in his mind the intended mental picture. There is one restriction: the impact of a literary work depends on the degree of comprehension and the level of aesthetic sense it calls for, for when a group of individuals are united in the same feeling for beauty this requires a deep awareness on their part of the means of attaining to beauty.

Yet the writer's raw material is the language of his social group, but his genius can be measured by the success with which he uses this common language to produce an aesthetic effect, just as a musician conveys his moods by the originality with which he organizes a range of sounds, or as a painter or sculptor exploits colours or lines to render his feeling for the beautiful, or as the architect Eupalinos constructed at Megara a little temple with four columns and in a very simple style, which was the mathematical image of a Corinthian girl he had loved.

Indo-European dialectology. In addition to the considerable contribution made by Bartoli and the neolinguists to the task of establishing and furthering the study of Indo-European dialectology, due recognition must also be given to the outstanding part played by Antoine Meillet. His book *Les dialectes indo-européens* (1908) was the first work devoted to the question as a whole. On the basis of a study of a series of phonetic, morphological and lexical parallels, he concluded that a distinction could be made between an eastern group and a western group (i.e. he reverted to the traditional distinction between *satəm* and *centum* languages).

On the other hand, the concept of intermediate units—hypothetical stages between common Indo-European and the known languages—was attacked by a German linguist, Walde, who in an article published in 1916 tried to show that the languages generally referred to as the *Italo-Celtic* group belonged in reality to two different groups, one consisting of Latin and Gaelic and the other of Osco-Umbrian and Brittonic. This of course was going too far, but it did serve to show how precarious were these notions that derived to all intents and purposes from Schleicher's *Stammbaum-theorie.*

Bartoli and the Italian linguists working along similar lines—the authoritative works in this field are those of Devoto, Bonfante (Bartoli's most faithful successor), Pisani and Terracini and those in which Bertoldi treated in masterly fashion the problems of substrata—suggested a flexible method of investigation for determining, by taking into account as many examples as possible from all aspects of linguistic structure, the criteria by which dialects should be classified. It was certainly rather daring to carry over into the field of the ancient Indo-European languages the methods of linguistic geography, that had first been applied to living dialects, that is, to a field in which it is possible to make on-the-spot investigations and constantly check one's results. The Indo-Europeanist, in fact, has only imperfect data on the early stages of the languages he is studying. Some dialects have come down to us only in the shape of paltry fragments or glosses, so that the scarcity of documentation deprives the available data of any great significance. Others, known only from sacred texts or inscriptions, provide only formulaic material of no great interest to the linguist. Even in the case of languages for which we appear to have a wealth of texts, such as Greek or Latin, it is clear that there are great gaps in our knowledge, including sometimes the ordinary everyday vocabulary or typical expressions of popular speech.

So, there was need for caution, which is why Bartoli, reacting in his turn against the dogmatism of the neogrammarians, at least in the most fruitful part of his researches,[169] did not consider his 'spatial norms' as laws operating mechanically and blindly, but on the contrary as guides to research, pointers to the method to be followed.

---

[169] For, after opposing so strenuously the doctrinaire attitude of the neogrammarians, Bartoli, in the latter part of his career, had come to have such blind confidence in the principles he had formulated as guides for linguistic research that he now considered them as a rigid framework of dogmas. The story of this drama of one man's intellectual life has been told by G. Devoto in an article written in Bartoli's memory (*Word*, III, 1947, 208–216).

The first thing to be done then is to analyse correctly and try to evaluate the correspondences between dialects. Some of these correspondences merely show that features of an older stage of the language have been preserved and are consequently archaisms. Others may be the result of independent but parallel developments. Others, finally, are innovations which, in a given dialectal group, show a common evolution (for example, in the notorious question of the treatment of the velars, the *satəm* languages are united by a common tendency to palatalize the velars whilst the *centum* languages, which merely preserve the sound existing at an earlier stage, are in this respect united by no characteristic feature).

It goes without saying that innovations are the significant features in determining dialectal relationships. Plotting on a map the isoglosses relating to such innovations is the best way to form an idea of the relationships between dialects and attempt to trace their history. The first task therefore is to find out what correspondences exist, but it is a very delicate undertaking to interpret them correctly and decide whether they are conclusive evidence that the dialects are cognate. Care must be taken, for example, not to interpret as innovations the results of parallel developments—it is not always easy to distinguish between these two kinds of relationship—or of reciprocal influences. Here we come up against the highly important problems of substrata, superstrata and linguistic borrowing (or adstrata). These questions arise principally in the study of vocabulary.

Finally, one must not lose sight of what might be called negative factors. The existence of striking and well-documented similarities should not blind us to the existence of far-reaching divergences that make it unlikely that two or more given dialects belong to the same group.

Another fruitful idea associated with the 'areal theory' (as it has sometimes been called, in view of the basic principles underlying it) is the combination of the factors of time and space. Introducing the dimension of time into the geographical framework made it possible to account for the paradoxical situation that arose when Tokharian and Hittite were deciphered. As we have seen,[170] the discovery of these languages did not, contrary to what had been expected, confirm the over-simple division of the Indo-European languages into two groups, a western one (the *centum* languages) and an eastern one (the *satəm* languages), but on the contrary revealed striking simi-

[170] P. 42.

larities between the newly-discovered languages and those of the extreme west of the Indo-European area. This confirmed a few isolated remarks that had already been made—but had never been followed up—on points of agreement between Italic and Celtic on the one hand and Indo-Iranian on the other.[171] It became clear that these were in fact cases of preservation, that the dialectal features that appear in 'lateral areas' (Meillet later spoke of 'marginal languages') generally belong to an older linguistic stratum than those of the central area. In other words, the points of agreement between languages that are geographically the furthest removed from one another are archaisms and not innovations, such as for example the impersonal forms of the verb in -r found in Latin (Type: itur, later extended to the medio-passive: fertur) and Celtic, and also in Hittite, Tokharian, Armenian and Phrygian, the subjunctive in -a- (Type: Old Latin tagam) that is characteristic of Italic, Celtic and Tokharian, the genitive in -i (Type: Latin lupi), forms corresponding to which also occur in Celtic and Sanskrit, and some striking points of lexical agreement amongst Italic, Celtic and Indo-Iranian, such as Latin rex and Sanskrit rájā, Latin flāmen and Sanskrit brahmá, etc. In this way, the relationship of the various dialects to Common Indo-European has been reinterpreted. To take the case of the classical languages, Latin is now seen as a conservative language many of whose features, hitherto thought to be innovations, are to be explained as vestiges of an archaic stage of Indo-European, whilst Greek belongs to a more innovating group. This is obviously of great importance for our whole conception of Indo-European.

What in fact is this original Indo-European (*Urindogermanisch*) that had been so patiently and so eruditely reconstructed by the neogrammarians and the structure of which—sound system, morphology, syntax, vocabulary—Brugmann and his followers had tabulated with the utmost precision? Is it anything other than a state of language constructed on the basis of a comparison that, in theory, took in all known Indo-European languages but in practice was founded essentially on Sanskrit and Greek, as these two languages were considered to be the most archaic of the Indo-European languages? It is now clear where the methodological flaw—of which we have seen all too many examples in the last thirty years—lies. It consists in comparing the newly-deciphered languages with this

[171] J. Vendryes, 'Les correspondances de vocabulaire entre l'indo-iranien et l'italo-celtique', in *Mémoires de la Société de Linguistique de Paris*, XX, 1918, 265–285.

Indo-European that was reconstructed on the basis of all the *other* Indo-European languages—i.e. excluding the new ones—and indeed, in some respects, on the basis of only two or three languages that are quite arbitrarily considered as being especially typical. So it is not in the least surprising that characteristically Hittite features, for example, do not appear in this reconstructed Indo-European. And what value can one place on hypotheses like those of Sturtevant who placed Hittite on the same level as Indo-European as it is usually thought of, and considered these two as separate branches of what he calls 'Indo-Hittite'? It is obvious that if Hittite and Tokharian had been discovered fifty years earlier, Brugmann's Indo-European would have looked very different.

It is perhaps appropriate to recall here briefly that it was the discovery of Hittite that enabled J. Kuryłowicz and É. Benveniste to elaborate, simultaneously but independently, their theses, the results of which agree in their essentials, on the structure of early Indo-European. Benveniste's *Origines*[172] is a fundamental work in the history of the comparative grammar of the Indo-European languages. After Bopp's *Conjugationssystem* of 1816 and Saussure's revolutionary *Mémoire* of 1878, Benveniste's book is a third milestone in the history of the comparative grammar of the Indo-European languages. He defines the root, more strictly than Saussure does, as being composed of three elements that always occur in the same order: consonant (i.e. a consonant in the strict sense of the word, or consonantal sonant) + vowel (i.e. the fundamental vowel *e* with its apophonous form *o*) + consonant,[173] and it is seen thereafter as the minimum meaningful and productive element. If this theory modifies in certain respects the traditional view of Indo-European morphology (it does away with nasal infixes and disyllabic roots, for instance), it also confirms *grosso modo* and in certain important respects (such as the role of the sonants and the *shwa* phonemes) the truly prophetic views put forward with astonishing lucidity by Saussure in 1878 as a working hypothesis. Structuralist ideas and their strict Cartesian logic have clearly played a part in thus renewing the study of early Indo-European. Here again we must refer to Benveniste who, in a series of brilliant works,[174]

---

[172] É. Benveniste, *Origines de la formation des noms en indo-européen*, Paris, 1935.

[173] The term *triliteral*, which is used in another sense (that of consonantal structure) in the description of the Semitic languages, should be avoided in this connection.

[174] Such as his *Noms d'agent et noms d'action en indo-européen*, Paris, 1948.

has shown how individual facts must be explained by being integrated into the system.

Mechanism and mentalism. We have already seen on a number of occasions[175] that American linguists took an active part in the development of linguistics and that they were way out in front in certain respects, such as the putting into practice of structuralist methods. The fact that they have carried out a considerable amount of research on the synchronic plane especially is largely due to the enormous task presented by the problem of recording the vast number of Amerindian tongues that still survive, a task that is all the more urgent as many of them are now dying out. It would therefore be arbitrary to refer to 'American linguistics' as an independent school, even though in a number of respects American linguists profess views that are rather different from those current in Europe. There was of course the lack of contact resulting from the last war, but quite apart from this fortuitous circumstance, there is also the fact that the *sui generis* structure of the indigenous languages of America—to which the grammatical framework inherited from classical Antiquity cannot be applied—poses some very special problems.[176]

One aspect however of transatlantic linguistic thinking has hardly spread beyond the United States, namely the quarrel that in recent decades has brought to grips the proponents of mechanistic and mentalistic theories of language (the journals *Language* and *Word* reflect *grosso modo* these opposing tendencies). The *mechanistic* or *behaviourist* approach, deriving from Bloomfield (there is a Bloomfieldian orthodoxy upheld by what has sometimes been called the Yale school—Bernard Bloch, Robert A. Hall, Jr., Z. S. Harris and others) is a positivist system that considers that language, just like other human activities, is a natural consequence of the actions and reactions of the different elements making up the human body. Taking the view that the meaning of a linguistic form is the situation in which it is uttered by a speaker, Bloomfield discounts it and concentrates exclusively on the formal side of language. *Mentalism*, on the other hand, the approach preferred by E. Sapir and on the whole

---

[175] V. sup., pp. 29, 80–82, 83–84, 98, et inf., pp. 123, 128–130, 140.
[176] R. A. Hall, Jr., 'American Linguistics, 1925–1950', in *Archivum Linguisticum*, III, 1951, 101–125 and IV, 1952, 1–16.

by R. Jakobson, is a psychological doctrine that considers that the variability of language is an effect of the action on physical factors of a spiritual force (will, reflection, emotivity, etc.) that operates on our nervous centres. As opposed to the behaviourists, Sapir, who had carried out linguistic investigations amongst the American Indians, held that the 'linguistic consciousness' of the speakers must be taken into account. We shall see,[177] on the other hand, how he anticipated structuralism in his attempt to classify the languages of the world.

By taking what is soundest in the two points of view, such a confrontation might well have proved fruitful for research, if the views expressed by the French psychologist Henri Delacroix had been borne in mind: 'Though it is largely mechanical, the evolution of language is nevertheless subtended by the requirement of meaning', and: language is 'the work of the whole man'.[178] As it happened, however, the discussions turned out to be disappointing and often sterile because of the intolerance and polemical spirit that more than once animated the discussions, reminding one of those between the equally irreconcilable realists and nominalists of mediaeval scholasticism. In any case, the interest has largely gone out of the controversy now that our American colleagues have fervently and often felicitously adopted structuralist theories. But one would also like to see the end of such intransigent attitudes as still remain.

Soviet linguistics. After the Revolution, Russian scholars, who had taken an active part in the different movements in comparative grammar and linguistics, were abruptly cut off from the outside world and for many years thereafter remained in isolation. One of them, Nikolai Marr, was given the responsibility of interpreting, in the field of linguistics, the teaching of the new regime. Marr, who as it happens had become known for his well-documented publications on the Caucasian languages, got bogged down in the insoluble problem[179] of the origin of language (in his view, articulate language gradually replaced gesture language, on the initiative of the sorcerers who ruled over the tribes) and began, after the fashion

---

[177] Pp. 128–130.
[178] H. Delacroix, Le langage et la pensée, 2nd ed., Paris, 1930, pp. 608–609.
[179] V. sup., pp. 24–26.

I

of the Italian Alfredo Trombetti[180] but on even shakier grounds and with no scientific basis for his claims, to preach the doctrine of the monogenesis of the languages of the world. The most astonishing thing is that, for some thirty years, these eccentric views could have constituted the doctrinal basis of Soviet linguistics. Rejecting the comparative and historical method, Marr preached his 'Japhetic' theory which, on a purely semantic basis, constructed a strange linguistic palaeontology: originally, there had been four elements, 'totem-words' so to speak, *sal, ber, yon* and *rosh*, which, by means of the permutations *sal/ ʐal/ tsal/ dal/ gal/*, etc., gave rise to all languages. Further, Marr insisted on the class character of language, going so far as to declare that the speech of the same social classes in different regions is typologically less varied than the speech of the different social classes within the same nation. Finally, he considered language as forming part of a superstructure that could be abruptly modified as a result of changes in the economic infrastructure, whence the notion of 'revolutionary leaps' and that of over-simplified correspondences between 'linguistic stages' and social states.

In June 1950 (Marr had died in 1934) in a famous interview he gave to *Pravda*, Stalin formally condemned Marr's theses which, he said, contradicted the whole trend of the history of peoples and languages. He restored to favour the traditional study of linguistic relationships which 'can be of great usefulness for studying the laws of linguistic development', and insisted on the relationship of the Slav 'nations'. Finally he declared that language is closely bound up with human activity as a whole, so that language develops and evolves very slowly within the fold of a given society.[181]

Various explanations have been given of this abrupt change of direction which amounts to a complete about-turn. It has been interpreted as being due to a sensible reaction from a scientifically untenable position, or to the influence of Georgian university circles into which Marr's pseudo-Marxist theories had apparently never penetrated, or perhaps to the political background (the Slav linguistic community having to help to strengthen the union of the

---

[180] As early as 1905, Trombetti had proposed to classify languages on the basis of a division into two main branches, a southern (Africa and Oceania) and a northern (Eurasia and America): a suggestive system certainly but one that is completely undemonstrable in view of the imprecision of the morphological and lexical parallels adduced; cf. his *Elementi di glottologia*, Bologna, 1922.

[181] The bibliography of this unusual episode is considerable; see L. L. Thomas, *The Linguistic Theories of N. Ja. Marr*, Berkeley, 1957.

Slav peoples around Russia). However this may be, we have not had long to wait for results. Our Russian colleagues are once again taking an active part in the work of linguistics and comparative grammar, clear proof that the tradition had not been broken and that scholars in Russian universities had continued to work according to sound scientific principles that they passed on to their pupils. Another encouraging sign is that there has been a diffusion of information and that a desire has grown up to make known, undistorted by polemical considerations, the results of linguistic research carried on outside the Soviet Union in the last thirty years or so.

As well as being in the forefront of research into applied linguistics (such as the problem of machine translation), the Russians have also retained an interest in the philosophy of language; so it is that phonology and the structuralist views found in Europe and particularly in America have stirred up sometimes lively discussions. If most Soviet scholars reproach structuralism with having lost sight of the social reality surrounding language and of thereby becoming an abstract, idealistic conceptualism, which is quite contrary to their own historical materialist standpoint,[182] others on the contrary show keen interest in the development of structuralist methods. In a general way, moreover, Marxist linguistics, which considers language as an expression of thought and the product of a collective group, holds that it must be studied in conformity with these two aspects and insists on the complexity of the linguistic phenomenon.[183]

The French linguist, Marcel Cohen, has attempted to spread Marxist theories in numerous well-written works of vulgarization. However, apart from a few slight differences in terminology, the views he expresses are on the whole in line with the classic French theories that consider the linguistic fact as being above all a social fact.[184]

[182] The same point of view is encountered in other eastern European countries; see for example, with reference to Czechoslovakia, V. Kopal's report 'L'état actuel des études linguistiques en Tchécoslovaquie', in *Lingua*, II, 1949, 226–236.

[183] The work of our Soviet colleagues and the differences of opinion amongst them are well reflected in the annual volumes of *Voprosy Yazykoznaniya* ('Questions of Linguistics') published by the Moscow Academy of Sciences, which are reviewed each year by R. L'Hermitte in the *Bulletin de la Société de Linguistique de Paris*. Cf. also *Current Trends in Linguistics*, ed. by Th. A. Sebeok, Vol. I, *Soviet and East European Linguistics*, The Hague, 1963.

[184] V. sup., p. 97.

Phonetics. Following Rousselot,[185] experimental phonetics came into being and developed as a result of the laboratory use of instruments that were constantly being better adapted to its purposes: the analysis and recording of the movements of the vocal cords, of the part played by the oral and nasal cavities, of the way in which the various speech organs function, the use of X-rays, etc. It has also been shown to have universal validity, as experiments have confirmed beyond all dispute that individual somatic features have no bearing on the differentiation of the phonic material. But especially in recent years phonetics has soared phenomenally. Whereas, in the first half-century of its existence, it had concentrated particularly on studying the act of speaking, it has now turned towards an analysis of the act of hearing. Starting from the data provided by acoustic physics and using the latest techniques, it has perfected apparatus for analysing, measuring and recording with great precision; some of these aids—such as *Visible Speech*—make it possible to split up the sound into the harmonic and the formants, others even aim—and this procedure is interesting as a control—at synthesizing speech: remarkable results have already been obtained, especially regarding vowels, and we may look forward to considerable further progress.

Phonetics then has developed into an autonomous discipline of considerable scope, and linguistics has much of value to learn from it: more accurate ways of analysing the basic elements of language, the mechanics of functional oppositions, the role of accent and tone, the analysis of rhythm, etc. Phonetics has also achieved spectacular results in the field of applied linguistics, such as the creation of audio-visual techniques: here the principles of structural analysis and the application of phonological procedures (such as commutations) have been decisive for working out methods for the more rapid teaching of modern languages.[186]

Linguistic typology. When, at the beginning of the modern period, interest was aroused in the diversity of human languages, manuals began to appear classifying the ever-increasing number of known

[185] V. sup., p. 36.
[186] A good general idea of the various tendencies of contemporary phonetics is provided by the *Proceedings of the Fourth International Congress of Phonetic Sciences* (held at Helsinki in 1961), The Hague, 1962.

languages according to their geographical distribution. But soon another criterion intervened: that of genetic (or genealogical) classification which tried, with varying degrees of success, to fit languages into families. We have seen how this notion, when applied to Indo-European and aided by a strict method, had given rise last century to comparative grammar and had led to an upsurge in linguistic science.

The successes obtained in the study of the Indo-European languages by the neogrammarian school had given them such confidence in the historical method that they believed they would one day be able to apply it to all languages. In the preface to the imposing volume, *Les Langues du Monde* (1924), edited by Antoine Meillet and Marcel Cohen, Meillet, after first carefully defining with his customary lucidity the limits of the method by pointing out that, once one leaves the domain of historical documentation and ventures on to that of reconstructing linguistic communities dating from before the period for which we have documents, any kind of demonstration is illusory, added that he was convinced that the comparative grammar of the Indo-European languages provided the model to be followed and that the only valid criterion for establishing relationship is that of the 'continuity of grammatical forms'. And so he took the view that it would eventually be shown that the majority of languages belong to a small group of clearly defined families, and he stated at the beginning of his preface: 'The only linguistic classification that is both useful and worth-while is the genealogical one, based on the history of languages.'[187]

However, new facts, such as a wider and deeper knowledge of the native languages of America and Africa and new methods of investigation, have shown that although the genetic method gives brilliant and convincing results when applied to Indo-European and, to a less extent, to other groups of languages, such as the Hamito-Semitic group, attempts to use it for classifying all the languages in the world, most of which have no history, have failed. Moreover, even in the favourable case of languages that have been known for some considerable length of time, the genetic method is valid only over a period between two known dates. The prehistory of language can only be the object of risky speculation, for imaginative minds are always at liberty if they so wish—and some have not

[187] The text is reproduced in Meillet's *Linguistique historique et linguistique générale*, II, Paris, 1936, pp. 53–69.

hesitated to avail themselves of this freedom!—to reconstruct hypothetical states of language common to several historically attested families (Indo-European and Semitic, for example),[188] so that, paradoxically, the genetic method when carried to extremes demonstrates that it is impossible to prove that any two languages are not related.[189]

Another source of complication is the fact that in the course of their history languages influence one another and that their vocabulary and even their structure may be modified by borrowings from other languages. If we take Latin, for example, and study its earliest known form, the Etruscan, Greek, Gaulish, Illyrian, Mediterranean and other elements that had come into it are referred to as foreign borrowings and are taken into account in any attempt to determine, for example, the relationship between Latin and the other Indo-European languages. But when we come to study Vulgar Latin, at the dawn of the Romance languages, these elements have been fully absorbed into the language and there is no reason to consider them as special cases. The very concept therefore of linguistic relationship is vague and open to different interpretations. Indeed the notion of linguistic affinity, *Sprachverwandtschaft*, as defended by Schuchardt, has turned out to be one of the most fruitful lines of linguistic research in recent decades. Careful study has gone into determining more precisely the reciprocal influences of neighbouring dialects, and the factors making for unity amongst sometimes very different languages in the same geographical and social context, in short, into bringing out the different ways in which languages are related because they are adjacent, as a result of osmosis: the *Sprachbund*.[190]

---

[188] H. Möller's and Cuny's efforts in this direction have met with no success. The extremes to which they took their attempts at reconstruction recall Schleicher's (except for the fact that they took the precaution of indicating unattested forms by means of asterisks). With the aid of a daring pattern of roots and suffixes they confronted the puzzled reader with algebraic-looking and mostly unpronounceable forms that are supposed to symbolize the common language the existence of which they are trying to prove.

[189] A. Meillet, *Linguistique historique et linguistique générale*, II, Paris, 1936, p. 55.

[190] In this connection see for example V. Pisani, 'Parenté linguistique', in *Lingua*, III, 1952, 3–16 (=*Saggi di linguistica storica*, Turin, 1959, pp. 29–42) and the reports by Giuliano Bonfante and Giacomo Devoto ('Il concetto di "lega linguistica" e la sua applicazione all' "indeuropeo" ') and Maurice Leroy ('Stratificazioni cronologiche nei rapporti fra le lingue indeuropee') in *Atti del III Convegno Internazionale di Linguisti* (*Milano, 1958*), Milan, 1961, pp. 39–79.—For the *Sprachverwandtschaft*, cf. *Hugo Schuchardt-Brevier*, edited by L. Spitzer (v. sup., p. 51, n. 7), pp. 189–204; the term *Sprachbund*

All this explains why Meillet's preface was not reprinted in the second edition (1952) of *Les Langues du Monde*. It would have been contradicted by the very contents of the volume. For, beside the grouping by families that remains the professed aim of the work and the geographical presentation that had been decided on wherever the genealogical method was not applicable, another principle, that of typological classification, can be seen timidly peeping through here and there, as in the case of the Amerindian languages. By a typological classification is meant a method which, without regard for the geographical situation of the languages in question or for genealogical relationships established on historical grounds, attempts to group languages according to structural features. In the particularly difficult task of classifying the thousands of dialects spoken throughout the world, the linguist will therefore be guided, without any preconceived ideas, i.e. without reference to previous classifications, by an analysis of the means of expression—phonetic, morphological, syntagmatic, semantic, rhythmic and so on—that are characteristic of each language.

We are of course still a long way from having established the universally valid criteria that would be acceptable to all those engaged on research on these lines and it cannot be denied that, in comparison with the well-ordered principles and scientific guarantees offered by the comparative grammar of the Indo-European languages, linguistic typology cuts a poor figure, but this is perhaps only an illusion or rather an error of perspective, for the objects of the two disciplines are totally different and it would be difficult to make a cool comparison between them. Nor is it surprising that American linguists have paid particular attention to developing this method and using it in their work. They are after all faced with an extremely complicated situation for which the methods of traditional linguistics have proved inadequate even when they are not in practice inapplicable, namely the extraordinarily rich and varied pattern of native languages of the three Americas (said to number about a thousand, if figures have any significance in this connection). And the

was proposed by N. S. Trubetzkoy at the Hague Congress of Linguists, 1928, cf. E. Schwyzer in *Zeitschrift für vergleichende Sprachforschung*, LXVIII, 1944, p. 98; R. Jakobson applies it to similarities of structure, distinguishing between *Sprachbünde* and *Sprachfamilien*: 'Sur la théorie des affinités phonologiques entre les langues', a paper read at the Fourth Congress of Linguists, Copenhagen, 1936, and reproduced as an appendix to Cantineau's French translation (1949) of Trubetzkoy's *Grundzüge*, pp. 351–365.

same problems face those who are concerned with the African languages or the 'primitive' languages of Oceania.

As a matter of fact, this typological method—apart perhaps from the word itself—is not all that recent or revolutionary. It could even be argued, as Benveniste has pointed out, that a genetic classification is also typological:[191] identifying forms and the elements of forms one with another—which is what historical linguistics sets out to do—makes it possible to work out the formal and grammatical structure characteristic of a given family. It has even been suggested that, inversely, it might be possible to base a genetic classification on purely typological criteria. This question, which is particularly important from the methodological point of view, was raised by Trubetzkoy in an article that appeared in 1939, a year after his death.[192] There is no one clear-cut answer. It seems obvious that the concepts of genetic relationship and typological relationship are independent, although in fact they are often superimposed one on the other; in other words, structural relationship may result from a common origin but it may also come about independently in several languages that are genetically unconnected.[193]

Moreover, differences in type seem so sharp that the idea of using 'typological' definitions to characterize certain groups of languages is as old as linguistic research itself. There was for example the parallel drawn by Humboldt between the language and mentality of a given people, or the notorious threefold classification first thought of by Schlegel and perfected by Schleicher. We have referred to the great success that this latter theory met with and also to the fact that in the long run little reliance could be placed on it.[194] Yet it must be recognized that this use of morphological criteria (isolating/agglutinative/inflecting) contains the germ of an idea that has made possible the elaboration of some of the best-constructed typological systems that have been proposed in the last fifty years, the underlying aim being to define a varying number of main types that would embrace all the systems that actually occur.

[191] É. Benveniste, 'La classification des langues', in Conférences de l'Institut de Linguistique de l'Université de Paris, XI, 1952–1953, p. 40.

[192] N. S. Trubetzkoy, 'Gedanken über das Indogermanenproblem', in Acta Linguistica, I, 1939, 81–89.

[193] Cf. R. Jakobson, 'Sur la théorie des affinités phonologiques entre les langues' (v. sup., p. 122, n. 190), pp. 352–353.

[194] V. sup., pp. 18–23.

One of the most interesting of such attempts and one of the best suited to serve as a starting point for later research was Finck's proposed classification (1909)[195] into eight types each defined by a characteristic language (which we shall indicate in parentheses): (a) *isolating*, comprising two types, *radical-isolating* (Chinese: monosyllabic, relationships being expressed by word order and 'empty words') and *stem-isolating* (Samoan, a Polynesian language: the use of suffixes and affixes, with particles playing a leading part); (b) *flexional*, comprising three types, *radical-flexional* (Arabic: modifications of the root), *stem-flexional* (Greek: modifications of the stem), and *group-flexional* (Georgian: inflected forms can themselves take affixes); (c) *affixal*, comprising three types, *subordinating* (Turkish: elements suffixed to the root), *incorporating* (Greenland Eskimo: a conglomeration of elements suffixed to the radical, whence a pronounced synthetism and the creation of lengthy words representing a whole sentence), and *seriant* (Subiya, a Bantu dialect: a language making use of classifiers).

Finck's proposed scheme, however detailed and potentially useful it may appear, is however far from complete. How for example are the countless Amerindian languages with their highly original structures to be fitted in? And it is surely significant that when the same author published at the same time a repertoire of the languages of the world,[196] he arranged them not according to his own typological scheme but according to an ethnographical grouping:[197] in this work, languages are in fact classified, on the basis of the races that speak them, into four types: Caucasian (including Indo-European), Mongol, American and Ethiopian (i.e. Africa and Oceania).

Nevertheless, Finck's typological system has provoked some useful comments. Lohmann discussed the connection between it and the theory of categories on the one hand[198] and linguistic

[195] Franz Nikolaus Finck, *Die Haupttypen des Sprachbaus*, Leipzig, 1909, 3rd ed. (unchanged), 1936.

[196] *Die Sprachstämme des Erdkreises*, Leipzig, 1909, 3rd ed. (unchanged), 1923.

[197] He followed in this respect the example of the attempts made last century by F. Müller to establish a parallel between ethnography and linguistics; after working out a classification of the races of mankind in which the appearance of the hair played an all-important part (*Allgemeine Ethnographie*, Vienne, 1873), Müller had published a massive treatise on linguistics (*Grundriss der Sprachwissenschaft*, 7 vols., Vienne, 1876–1888) in which the same somatic criterion served to classify languages!

[198] J. Lohmann, 'M. Heideggers ontologische Differenz und die Sprache', in *Lexis*, I, 1948, 49–106; 'Sein und Zeit, Sein und Wahrheit in der Form der Sprache', ibid., II, 1959, 104–143.

geography on the other.[199] Scherer proposed a four-fold distribution on the basis of sentence construction, but he does so only very briefly and does not go into any detailed justification for this approach: however, it would be worth putting to the test.[200]

Finck's typology was also taken up with certain modifications by Ernst Lewy, who applied it to eighteen modern European languages selected as being particularly significant.[201] Within this limited field it produced extremely interesting results. This 'geographico-typological' grouping, as the author calls it, appeals to structural not to genetic criteria, i.e. it discounts history and at the same time helps to bring out the notion of *Sprachbund* referred to above.[202] Lewy divides the languages of Europe into five zones, each characterized by a different type, viz.: the *Atlantic*: flexion-isolating[203] (Basque, Spanish, French, Italian, Irish, English, Swedish); *Central*: word flexioning (German, Hungarian); *Balkan*: 'demonstrative' or correcting[204] (Albanian, Rumanian, Greek); *Eastern*: stem-flexioning and subordinating (Lettish, Russian, Finnish, Cheremiss and Mordvin); and *Arctic*: fully subordinating (Yurak, a Samoyed dialect).

It must be admitted that none of these typological classifications is wholly satisfactory. Finck's table, for example, with its eight classes, is not sufficiently rigorous and has serious gaps. It would be difficult in particular to fit into it dialects like those of the Sudan or the Amerindian languages that strike us as very strange. In fact, we all too often approach these languages with conceptions that are valid only for Indo-European languages. We must not lose sight of the fact that the development of scientific linguistics started with the study of Indo-European languages, and so there is a constant danger of applying to all languages methodological principles that are valid for Indo-European languages but which do not on that account necessarily have a universal value. This calls for some explanation.

---

[199] 'Sprachgeographie und Sprachtypologie', in *Lexis*, IV, 1955, 87–98.

[200] H. Güntert, *Grundfragen der Sprachwissenschaft*, 2nd ed. by A. Scherer, Heidelberg, 1956, pp. 116–117.

[201] Ernst Lewy, 'Der Bau der europäischen Sprachen', in *Proceedings of the Royal Irish Academy*, XLVIII, Section C, 1942–1943, 15–117.

[202] P. 122.

[203] [The English terms used here are taken from the summary in English appended to Lewy's article.]

[204] [The German terms used by Lewy with reference to this group are 'deutend, anreihend, berichtigend', op. cit., § 203, p. 67.]

That the distinction between noun and verb is one of the essential characteristics of Indo-European and the Indo-European languages emerges clearly from a study of these languages at all periods of their history and in all their forms (though English is somewhat embarrassing in this respect)[205] and attempts have been made to interpret the dichotomy object/process expressed by the opposition noun/verb as one of the logical foundations of the human mind. But in many languages there is no clear dividing line between noun and verb, in others the distinction is not made at all: some Amerindian languages for example use active or passive verb forms as 'nouns' and 'conjugate' particles. In Benveniste's words, 'the distinction between process and object appears essential only if one reasons on the basis of the classifications of one's native language and takes these as data having universal validity; and if those who insist on this distinction are asked to justify it, they will soon have to admit that if "horse" is an object and "to run" is a process, the reason is that one is a noun and the other a verb. A definition that tries to find a "natural" justification for the way a particular language organizes its notions is doomed to argue in a circle.'[206]

To take another example: it has always been accepted that one of the decisive criteria for determining the membership of a given linguistic family was the fact that the numerals remained intact and this feature is clearly shown in the Indo-European languages throughout the 4,000 years of their history and in a wide range of dialects, cases of substitution, the use of other forms and borrowings from other dialects being in fact extremely rare (examples are French *soixante dix* replacing *septante* 'seventy' and *quatre-vingts* replacing *octante* 'eighty', and Rumanian *o sută* 'a hundred' borrowed presumably from Slavic, cf. Old Slavic *sŭto*). It has been shown, however, that in other types of languages, numerals and even whole series of numerals have been borrowed for reasons that are not always apparent.[207] So the stability of the numerals in Indo-European is not a universal feature immanent in numerical systems but is probably due to particular causes such as the fact that the bartering of goods developed very late in the Indo-European world.[208]

---

[205] V. sup., p. 22.

[206] É. Benveniste, 'La phrase nominale', in *Bulletin de la Société de Linguistique de Paris*, XLVI, 1950, p. 20.

[207] Cf. M. Swadesh, 'Mosan I: A problem of Remote Common Origin', in *International Journal of American Linguistics*, XIX, 1953, 31–35.

[208] Cf. É. Benveniste, 'La classification des langues' (v. sup., p. 124, n. 191), p. 36.

The insufficiency and inadequacy of the grammatical framework drawn up for Indo-European—and even within these limits the traditional terminology is often imperfect—become all too obvious when we try and treat it as if it had universal validity. To take for example parts of speech or grammatical categories: if we apply traditional terminology to some Amerindian languages we find that we have pronouns that conjugate or personal forms of the verb that fall within the declensional system—the absurdity is only an apparent one, the mistake being to confer on the concepts 'noun' and 'verb' as they appear in Indo-European (and, of course, certain other languages) a universal value they do not possess. In fact, we still all too often study the languages of the world on the basis of notions derived from those languages we are familiar with; but, as É. Benveniste has shown, since the linguist's horizon has broadened, since the analysis of so-called 'primitive' languages has revealed 'a highly differentiated and systematic organization', the Indo-European type 'far from constituting a norm comes to look somewhat exceptional'.[209]

We must now turn to the great American linguist Edward Sapir's remarkable book *Language* (1921).[210] In addition to having a lucid mind and an extensive knowledge of Amerindian tongues,[211] Sapir (who died in 1939) was also deeply interested in the human value of the facts of language and in their aesthetic side[212] (he also, incidentally, wrote a number of poems). In Ch. VI of his book (which is written in a lively and often deliberately ironic or humorous style), he proposes a classification of linguistic types which marks an undeniable advance on previous schemes and, it might be said paradoxically, on those proposed later. He refers to three criteria:

First, the types of *concept* expressed (examined in his Ch. V), for which he suggests the following scheme: 'I. *Basic (Concrete) Concepts* (such as objects, actions, qualities) . . . II. *Derivational Concepts* (less concrete, as a rule, than I, more so than III): normally expressed by

[209] 'Tendances récentes en linguistique générale' (v. sup., p. 84, n. 81), p. 133.

[210] Edward Sapir, *Language: an Introduction to the Study of Speech*, New York and Oxford, 1921; paperback ed., London, n.d. (c. 1963).

[211] He did not, however, neglect the Indo-European languages or decry their importance as did his pupil B. L. Whorf, with his characteristic lack of any sense of proportion; cf. G. Mounin, 'A propos de *Language, Thought and Reality* de Benjamin Lee Whorf', in *Bulletin de la Société de Linguistique de Paris*, LVI, 1961, 122–138.

[212] The following sentence from his preface (p. iii) is typical: 'Among contemporary writers of influence on liberal thought Croce is one of the very few who have gained an understanding of the fundamental significance of language'.

affixing non-radical elements to radical elements or by inner modification of these . . . III. *Concrete Relational Concepts* (still more
abstract, yet not entirely devoid of a measure of concreteness) [e.g.
numerals, gender] . . . IV. *Pure Relational Concepts* (purely abstract):
. . . serve to relate the concrete elements of the proposition to each
other, thus giving it definite syntactic form'.[213] It is to be noted that
concepts of Type I are normally expressed by independent words,
whilst II and III are expressed either by affixes (suffixes, prefixes,
infixes) or by internal modification of radical elements (such as the
principle of alternation); Type IV uses all these possibilities together
with word order.

Second, the criterion of *technique*, i.e. 'the formal processes most
typically developed in the language',[214] which, according to the
author, can be *isolating, agglutinative, fusional* or *symbolic*, the latter
type being those languages that 'possess the power to change the
significance of the radical elements by internal changes (reduplica-
tion; vocalic and consonantal change; changes in quantity, stress,
and pitch)'.[215]

Third, there is the type of *synthesis* that characterizes the language.
According to this criterion languages can be designated *analytic* (here
one can distinguish between languages that do not combine concepts
into single words at all, such as Chinese, and those that do so
economically, such as English and French), or *synthetic* (such as Latin,
Arabic and Finnish) or *polysynthetic* (i.e. 'more than ordinarily
synthetic'; in such languages, e.g. the Algonkin dialects, 'the
elaboration of the word is extreme').[216]

At first sight, this would seem to be the old concept of tripartition
once again, but without the intransigence that characterized it
last century and rethought in the light of new knowledge. In reality,
Sapir took account of the complexity (that he was well aware of) of
linguistic data and the four *basic types* (A, B, C, D) that he finally
tries to set up are the result of combining the various criteria listed
above. So, Chinese, having an isolating technique and an analytic
'synthesis', appears as a combination of the concept types I and IV,
which in general characterizes group A; Turkish falls into group B
because it combines types I, II and IV and is furthermore charac-

[213] Sapir, *Language*, pp. 106–107; paperback ed., p. 101.
[214] Ibid., p. 133; paperback ed., p. 126.
[215] Ibid., p. 133; paperback ed., p. 126.
[216] Ibid., p. 135; paperback ed., p. 128.

terized by an agglutinative technique and a synthetic 'synthesis'; and so on.

The resulting table is in no way absolute, the compartments are by no means watertight and weakened forms of the processes concerned and secondary characteristics are frequently indicated by means of data presented in parentheses. Further, if every language in the world is to be fitted into the table, this has nothing whatsoever to do with any geographical or genetic factors (French and Latin for example fall into different categories). Sapir was too well aware of the weaknesses and gaps in his theory to take it as anything more than a provisional scheme that might well call for revision. It must be recognized that the various criteria require delicate handling, as the interpretation of a given linguistic phenomenon often depends on the largely subjective judgment of the linguist. Furthermore, many languages are marked by several different characteristics and so do not fit neatly into any one category. Sapir himself is doubtful and hesitant at times. He classes Latin, Greek and Sanskrit, for example, amongst the synthetic languages but with reservations regarding technique which he considers to be fusional but with a 'symbolic tinge'. And he makes the shrewd comment: 'Languages, after all, are exceedingly complex historical structures. It is of less importance to put each language in a neat pigeon-hole than to have evolved a flexible method which enables us to place it, from two or three independent standpoints, relatively to another language.'[217]

This classification, in spite of its subjective aspects and the hesitations it allows, is certainly the best argued and most pragmatic yet proposed on these lines, i.e. according to what might be termed a purely linguistic or, so to speak, 'structural'[218] method. Sapir examines the data according to exclusively linguistic criteria, taking account both of the semantic basis of the language and of its way of expressing it (i.e. of both substance and form). Although Saussure is not actually mentioned in *Language*, this approach is in keeping with the famous apocryphal dictum in the *Cours*: 'The one and only true object of linguistics is language envisaged in and for itself'.

And yet it seems that this method has now reached its fullest extent, and that no more concrete results can be expected from

217 Ibid., p. 149; paperback ed., p. 140.

218 [The French text uses the word *structurel* which is commented on in a footnote thus: 'We use the term *structurel* and not *structural* as the latter is now applied only to the movements that, as we have seen, are grouped together under the label of *structuralism*.'

it. Therefore, we must turn to the perspectives opened up some years ago by É. Benveniste's examination of the problem of the classification of languages.[219] 'Languages,' he observes, 'are such complex organisms (*ensembles*) that they can be classified in function of a large number of criteria. Any consistent and comprehensive typology must take account of several kinds of distinguishing factors and draw up a hierarchy of the pertinent morphological features.' Noting the difficulties that all typological classifications hitherto proposed have come up against, Benveniste wonders whether it should not be first acknowledged that form is merely the possibility of structure. Consequently, the most pressing task is to work out a general theory of linguistic structure and the attempt at classification should in this case bear on the elements of this structure. He continues: 'The initial condition for such an undertaking would be to abandon the principle—which has never been formulated and yet weighs all the more heavily on much of present-day linguistics since it seems so obvious—that the only significant thing in linguistics is the data, that language is wholly contained in its actual manifestations'. He then adds: 'The linguistic datum is a result and we must find out what it is a result of'. It appears therefore that the only way we can arrive at a rational classification of this kind is by having recourse, in order to formulate definitions adequately and define relationships correctly, to the procedures of symbolic logic. It is interesting to note that at the 1957 Oslo Congress the discussion on typology showed that 'the system, and not the inventory, must serve as a basis for typology'.[220]

In other words, to use the vocabulary of one of the aspects of structural linguistics that has been the most intelligently worked out, we transcend the form to appeal to the function. Recalling what was said above[221] with reference to structuralism, we may add that such a *logico-linguistic method* should be handled only by experienced researchers well acquainted with traditional methods of comparison; research into the classification of languages must not give renewed currency to the myth of language considered as a being having an existence of its own independent of human contingencies; we must

[219] V. sup., p. 124, n. 191.
[220] Paul L. Garvin, *Proceedings of the Eighth International Congress of Linguists*, Oslo, 1958, p. 25, opening the discussion on R. Jakobson's report on the topic 'What can typological studies contribute to historical comparative linguistics?', ibid., pp. 17–24.
[221] Pp. 77–78.

not lose contact with reality. With these safeguards, the method should prove fruitful.

Stylistics. Although stylistics is rather on the fringe of linguistics, it deserves to be mentioned here because of the important place it occupies in the history of linguistics, by virtue both of the impetus it has frequently received from linguistics and of the instructive contribution it has made to it. In reality, the term is applied to very varied types of research. If we leave aside the traditional study of style, which consists of a whole range of heterogeneous and subjective remarks relating both to form and to subject-matter and complying with no very clearly-defined norms—'the criticism of a *littérateur* or an *honnête homme* rather than of a grammarian'[222]—the basic distinction today is between the stylistic study of the expressive resources of a language (*stylistique de l'expression*) and the stylistic study of an individual writer (*stylistique de l'individu*).

The former, which within the Saussurian school was defined by Bally as the study of the affective elements of language, is synchronic and forms part of the problem of the distinction between *langue* and *parole*.[223] Bally and his followers sought to classify the stylistic value of the means of expression and to determine the reasons for the speaker's choice of such and such an expression. In contrast to this approach, which is concerned with language as the means of expression of a linguistic community, linguists of the idealist school, the followers of Croce or Vossler (Vossler had also been much influenced by Schuchardt) study the stylistics of the individual, which is concerned especially with facts of *parole* and the relationship between the expression and the speaker who uses it.[224] This then is a genetic study concerned primarily with the literary language and it is the source of very many works on the style of various writers. This regeneration of literary criticism owes much to one of Vossler's pupils, Leo Spitzer. In reality, these two conceptions of stylistics are not incompatible: one can in fact study the way in which the expressive resources of a language are used in the composition of a work of art.[225]

[222] P. Guiraud, *La stylistique*, Paris, 1954, p. 41; this little volume provides a useful introduction to the problems of stylistics.
[223] V. sup., p. 62.
[224] V. sup., pp. 103.
[225] Cf. for example S. Ullmann, *Style in the French Novel*, Cambridge, 1957 (2nd ed., Oxford, 1964), pp. 1–37.

Semantics. Finally, we turn to one of the most remarkable of recent developments in linguistics, the renewal of semantics, the latest and by no means the least fruitful extension of the work of Saussure.

Semantics, which was created by Bréal, had grown up as a historical science the essential objective of which was to study the evolution of the meanings of words: how words change their meanings, and ideas their expression.[226] Semantics so envisaged has produced numerous valuable works devoted to various evolutionary processes in various languages.[227] The crowning achievement of this kind of historical research was the publication in 1952 of Heinz Kronasser's *Handbuch der Semasiologie*. This richly documented volume follows in the classic tradition since it deals essentially with changes of meaning. Kronasser's attempt to determine the psychological motivations accounting for the different processes bringing about change of meaning—he expresses the view that a clear distinction between psychology and linguistics would definitely be harmful—is of course somewhat subjective and to be accepted only with caution. These motivations do no more after all than recall the logical point of view inherited from the rhetoric of antiquity and mediaeval scholasticism and the teachings of general grammar based on Cartesian principles.

We have seen how the analyses proposed in the *Cours* led to the structuralist theories which, applied first of all to the study of sounds, soon broadened their scope and gradually took in the fields of morphology and syntax and were finally applied to linguistic structure as a whole—with the exception of semantics which stood outside these developments. 'This time-lag,' to quote Ullmann, 'is due to the particular nature of lexical data. The phonological and grammatical system of a language is made up of a small number of elements; the vocabulary, on the other hand, commands resources so vast as to be virtually innumerable. . . . To this quantitative contrast are added important differences in quality. Phonological and grammatical elements are in most cases closely organized and relatively stable in a given state of the language, whereas the vocabulary is essentially unstable: it is constantly enriched with new words while others fall into disuse or are given new meanings.'[228]

---

[226] V. sup., pp. 37–39.
[227] Cf. p. 39, n. 45.
[228] S. Ullmann, 'Orientations nouvelles en sémantique', in *Journal de Psychologie*, LV, 1958, p. 341.

K

The effect of this special character of the meaningful elements of language, which appears to render them unamenable to any rigid classification, had been that some extreme (or, rather, doctrinaire) manifestations of American structuralism—here one sees a still-active antimentalism at work—have deliberately chosen, on the pretext of scientific accuracy, to exclude these meaningful elements from their research. This is particularly true of the previously mentioned[229] manuals of general linguistics by Bloch and Trager and by Harris.

In 1951, S. Ullmann published his *Principles of Semantics*, the essential merit of which is that it applies to semantics the techniques of structural investigation and presents the facts in the form of a very clearly written manual. For this new approach had been foreshadowed and prepared by a number of precursors whose work had not thitherto received the attention it deserved, or not from linguists at least. In 1921 L. Roudet, working under the influence of psychological linguistics, distinguished between those semantic changes in which a word acquires a different meaning, e.g. French *plume* [which means first 'feather' and then 'pen'], and those in which the meaning is transferred from one word to another, e.g. French *pas*[230] [i.e. in the construction *ne . . . pas* in which the negative idea that was originally expressed by *ne* has been assumed by *pas*, which originally had a positive value (< *passum*), e.g. *pas du tout* 'not at all' or colloquial *Je viens pas* for *Je ne viens pas* 'I'm not coming']. Ten years later in a study dealing with English, G. Stern made a similar distinction between 'changes due to external, non-linguistic causes' and 'changes due to linguistic causes' and proposed for the latter a somewhat complicated table of shifts of meaning.[231]

But the most lucid attempt was that made by Jost Trier who conceived of the notion of the 'linguistic field'. This notion, forming a link between the plane of concepts and that of expression, appears as a kind of 'sprachliche Zwischenwelt' and makes for a clearer understanding of the relationships between *signifiant* and *signifié* that had also exercised philosophers such as Cassirer and Carnap.

[229] P. 80 and n. 60 and 61.—N.B. also Martinet's doubts concerning semantics; see his *Éléments de linguistique générale* (v. sup., p. 83), pp. 40–41, English translation, pp. 42–43.

[230] L. Roudet, 'Sur la classification psychologique des changements sémantiques', in *Journal de Psychologie*, XVII, 1921, 676–692.

[231] G. Stern, *Meaning and Change of Meaning, with Special Reference to the English Language*, Göteborg, 1931; new ed., Bloomington, 1964.

Trier developed his idea of the 'linguistic field' on the basis of a typical example taken from German.[232] His thesis is summarized by Ullmann[233] as follows:

'[Trier compares] the basic structure of the intellectual field in Middle High German around 1200 and a century later. In the first period, the field was organized around three key-terms: *wîsheit*, *kunst* and *list*. In Modern German these mean respectively "wisdom", "art" and "cunning, craft, trick", but to the contemporary speaker they had a totally different meaning and significance. They embodied two fundamental principles of mediaeval civilization: feudalism and universality. The feudal principle was expressed in the distinction between *kunst* and *list*: the former referred to courtly and chivalric attainments, the latter to skills which fell outside the courtly sphere. Universality was ensured by *wîsheit* which could act as an alternative for both *kunst* and *list* and also as a global term denoting human wisdom in all its aspects, theological as well as mundane.

A very different picture emerges from the German mystical vocabulary around 1300, which was investigated by one of Trier's pupils. First of all, the terms themselves are different: *wîsheit*, *kunst* and *wizzen*. *List* has dropped out of the intellectual sphere since the pejorative components of its meaning had cast a shadow on its more reputable uses; on the other hand, the substantivized infinitive *wizzen* has joined the key-terms of the field. But it is not simply a case of replacing one word by another: the structure of the field, and the whole philosophy behind it, have radically altered. The two pillars on which the earlier system rested have crumbled away. Feudalism has disintegrated, and the distinction between courtly and non-courtly attainments has become superfluous and even meaningless. The catholicity of the earlier outlook has also been lost: *wîsheit* is no longer a general term covering the whole range of human wisdom, but is now reserved for religious and mystical experiences. Meanwhile the pair *kunst - wizzen* shows an incipient distinction between knowledge and art.'

This is in line with Saussure's view that the elements of a language mutually determine one another's value: any change in the value of a

---

[232] Jost Trier, *Der deutsche Wortschatz im Sinnbezirk des Verstandes*, Heidelberg, 1931.
[233] [This summary of Trier's thesis is taken from S. Ullmann's *Semantics: an Introduction to the Science of Meaning*, Oxford, 1962, pp. 248–249, and replaces the somewhat briefer account given in the original French text.]

concept entails a modification in the values of related concepts and, of course, ultimately, these changes in the content of the concepts are reflected in the corresponding words. Synchrony and diachrony could not have been more harmoniously united. In fact, even before structuralism was established on firm foundations, Trier's theory— which is truly remarkable at least in so far as it relates to the intellectual vocabulary (the affective and technical aspects, etc., are left out of account)—applied structuralist methods to semantics and foreshadowed the way in which semantics was to be completely transformed twenty years later.

Another theory which is less revolutionary, as it related to vocabulary rather than structure and was limited to purely semantic relationships, is that of *associative fields* put forward by Ch. Bally.[234] The word *bœuf* 'ox' for example evokes the ideas of (i) 'cow, bull, calf', etc., (ii) 'tillage, plough', etc., and (iii) those of strength, stamina, slowness, etc. (cf. proverbial expressions such as *un vent à décorner les bœufs* or phrases like *ruminer une idée* 'to ruminate over an idea'). In this way, Bally was merely making explicit, but also restricting the scope of, Saussure's idea of 'constellations' of 'associative relationships'. The *Cours* distinguished various types of association according to whether the common element is the stem (*enseignement/ enseigner/ enseignons*, . . .), the suffix (*enseignement/ armement/ changement*, . . .) or whether the association depends on related *signifiés* (*enseignement/ instruction/ apprentissage*, . . .) or on the fact that the acoustic images have something in common (*enseignement* [in which *-ment* < *-mentum* is a suffix used for forming nouns from verbs] */ justement* [in which *-ment* < *mente* is an adverbial suffix]).

Starting from considerations of this kind, S. Ullmann, after first distinguishing between changes due to linguistic conservatism (Stern's 'changes due to external, non-linguistic causes') and those due to linguistic innovation, notes that in the latter case we may have either transfer of name or transfer of sense and that this transfer operates as a result either of similarity or of contiguity. He therefore constructs a scheme taking account of all the possible types of association. In this way, then, the structuralist semanticist of today sometimes constructs diagrams strangely reminiscent of the subdivisions of the rhetoric of antiquity. This is found in Ullmann's chapter on historical semantics, for the *Principles* contain a descrip-

234 'L'arbitraire du signe', in *Le français moderne*, VIII, 1940, p. 195.

tive part and a historical part as the author is one of those who, like H. Frei, accept Saussure's antinomy between synchrony and diachrony. He considers that the contrast between these two ways of looking at language is obvious and that both are equally legitimate, adding: 'What is not, is the combination of both points of view, the introduction of historical data into the description of a language'. And he quotes Bally's witty formula that one might as well build up a portrait of a man from photographs taken at different ages, with a baby's mouth, an adult's beard and an old man's wrinkles.[235] And if Ullmann foresees the possibility of constructing a system of panchronistic semantics—the term *panchronique* itself derives from Saussure—having as its task to determine what is common to all languages and all periods of time, he conceives of it, following a suggestion of Sommerfelt's,[236] as having the binary form pansynchronistic/pandiachronistic.

It is obvious that the distinction between synchrony and diachrony is useful as a didactic procedure for describing and exploring the data,[237] but it is certainly going too far to turn this distinction into a *sine qua non* of semantic study. We hasten to add that Ullmann himself recognizes elsewhere that some attenuation of the antinomy is called for and that 'there are cases where a combination of the two methods is more fruitful than their strict separation'.[238]

The fact of the matter is that any structure, whatever the level or period of the language we elect to study, is the result of historical developments an understanding of which contributes greatly to explaining its configuration at any given time. Furthermore, unless it is to fall into the same 'atomistic' errors as the neogrammarians, the history of meanings cannot be based on isolated words. It is essential to examine the way in which the whole structure of which they are an integral part (the 'semantic field') evolves. A classic

---

[235] 'Orientations nouvelles en sémantique' (v. sup., p. 133, n. 228), p. 340.

[236] *Principles of Semantics*, pp. 264–266.

[237] Vendryes pertinently observes that, in addition to traditional *etymology* which is essentially diachronic (to draw up the etymology of a word is to trace its history by finding out its early forms and working back as far as the existing documents allow) and popular etymology which explains changes in the form of the word by the attraction exerted by similar words, there is room for a *static etymology* which, for the grouping of words, would appeal both to their evocative value and to other factors such as their relative frequency, their social, technical and intellectual level, etc.: 'Pour une étymologie statique', in *Bulletin de la Société de Linguistique de Paris*, XLIX, 1953, 1–19.

[238] *Précis de sémantique française*, 2nd ed., Berne, 1959, p. 41.

example is that of Latin *coxa* 'hip' which gives French *cuisse* 'thigh'. Merely to call this an example of 'shift of meaning' as Kronasser does[239] (similarly *bucca* 'cheek' > *bouche* 'mouth') in no way serves to account for the process: Wartburg has skilfully elucidated this difficult case[240] and Ullmann himself has taken it up in a study that implicitly marks a change from his previous position on this point,[241] and it emerges that the word must be considered as a member of a group, when it can be seen that there is a change of terminology in respect of all three of hip, thigh and leg, and that no one of these changes can be explained without reference to the other two. The change therefore affects not merely *coxa* but the whole semantic field of which it is a part, and the explanation of the change *coxa* > *cuisse* is not that it is a simple association of contiguity, a case of metonymy, but is to be found by studying the whole lexical system it belongs to. Is there any need to emphasize that attention had already been drawn to this interpenetration of the elements of the system in cases such as this by Gilliéron who can therefore be said to have anticipated structuralism?

The fact that so many valuable works on semantics have been published in the course of the last ten years shows that there was ample justification for calling in structuralist methods to bring about a timely revival of the study of semantics and there have been a number of different approaches to the problem.

It is particularly significant that, at the 1957 Oslo Congress,[242] the report on the question: 'To what extent can meaning be said to be structured?' was drawn up by Louis Hjelmslev himself. Defining the programme of structural semantics, he said: 'To introduce the notion of *structure* into the study of semantics is to introduce the notion of *value* as well as that of *meaning*'. And he showed by a few examples how the notions of commutation and

---

[239] *Handbuch der Semasiologie*, p. 85.

[240] W. von Wartburg, *Einführung in Problematik und Methodik der Sprachwissenschaft*, 2nd ed., 1962, pp. 117–118 (French trans., *Problèmes et méthodes de la linguistique*, 2nd ed., 1963, p. 127).

[241] 'Historical Semantics and the Structure of the Vocabulary', in *Miscelánea Homenaje a André Martinet*, Vol. I, La Laguna, 1957, pp. 289–303.

[242] It is indicative of the lack of interest in semantics amongst linguists over a long period that the International Congresses of Linguists, from the first (The Hague, 1928) to the sixth (Paris, 1948) ignored it. The London Congress of 1952 (the one before the Oslo Congress) marked the change, one of its plenary sessions being devoted to the problem of meaning: *Proceedings of the Seventh International Congress of Linguists*, London, 1956, pp. 3–17 and 179–233.

substitution, which are a familiar part of the reasoning of the glossematicians, can be brought into semantic analysis.[243]

P. Guiraud has given some excellent examples of the way in which the explanation of reputedly obscure words can be facilitated by considering the word as part of the system to which it belongs, as part of the pattern of forms and senses that make up what he calls its *morpho-semantic field*.[244]

G. Matoré's *lexicologie*[245] which, although comparatively recent in origin, has already inspired some remarkable studies of the vocabulary of French, is in line with the French sociological school since it is defined by Matoré as 'a sociological discipline using the linguistic material of words'. Its originality is that it tackles the problem by using the resources of structural method and studying words as part of a whole, namely by picking out the 'witness words' (*mots-témoins*) and the 'key words' (*mots-clés*) that are characteristic of a given society (so, for example, *magasin* which around 1820-25 tends to replace *boutique*, or *bourgeois* which in the 1830s must be studied together with its corollaries *prolétaire, artiste*, etc.). This study of *notional fields* is not so very different from Trier's approach and Guiraud has admirably stated their respective positions: 'Professor Trier studies first and foremost the spiritual and moral side of life in order to recapture the "spirit" of a nation and a period, whereas M. Matoré is principally interested in the material, economic, technical and political substratum of the vocabulary'.[246]

---

[243] *Proceedings of the Eighth International Congress of Linguists*, Oslo, 1958, pp. 636–654 (reprinted in L. Hjelmslev, *Essais linguistiques*, Copenhagen, 1959, pp. 96–112, under the title 'Pour une sémantique structurale').

[244] *Bulletin de la Société de Linguistique de Paris*, LII, 1956, 265–288, and LVII, 1962, p. 103, n.1.—In his little volume, *La sémantique*, Paris, 1955, P. Guiraud sets out clearly, if sometimes with excessive schematization, the different ways of looking at semantics. A good bibliographical survey is also to be found in K. Baldinger's *Die Semasiologie*, Berlin, 1957, but the most recent introduction to the problems of semantics is S. Ullmann's *Semantics, an Introduction to the Science of Meaning*, Oxford, 1962, in which the author reviews the present state of research.

[245] *La méthode en lexicologie: Domaine français*, Paris, 1953.—Matoré considers that lexicology, a sociological discipline, 'envisages groups of words considered statistically from the notional point of view' in contradistinction to semantics which 'studying as it does the successive values of words considered individually, belongs to the field of historical linguistics'. This attitude was quite understandable at the time Matoré's book was published (1953), but is now out of date. There is no reason at all why one should not speak of structural semantics as well as of historical semantics, and this is all to the good as this marks a return to a more general interpretation of M. Bréal's original definition of semantics as 'the science of meanings'.

[246] P. Guiraud, *La sémantique*, p. 75.

What contribution finally can statistical methods make to semantics? Word lists and frequency counts have been extensively used by philologists and linguists, especially for the exegesis of literary works, ever since Antiquity (one need only think of the γλῶσσαι of the Alexandrian grammarians). But it is only recently that mathematical methods have been systematically applied to language, particularly following the publication of the works of G. K. Zipf[247] whose formulae cannot fail to disturb linguists, such as for example the following referring to the relationship between polysemy and frequency of use: 'The different meanings of a word will tend to be equal to the square root of its relative frequency.'

A further occasion for scepticism arises from the difficulty most linguists experience in following and checking the reasonings of the statisticians. We have cause to be grateful to those of our colleagues who have taken the trouble to initiate themselves into the mysteries of statistics and to explain the lessons to be learned therefrom in terms that can be understood by any linguist who is prepared to make the effort. Guiraud, for example, has interested himself both in the statistics of vocabulary and in information theory, which might well provide a general method applicable not only to semantics but also to phonology and morphology.[248] But one wonders whether there is not an element of risk in applying to the study of the meaningful value of words a logical method that is relevant essentially to the formal aspects of the elements of language. The reservations we expressed above[249] concerning the attempt to resort to communication theory to account for the relationship between *langue* and *parole* are all the more applicable here.

[247] *Human Behavior and the Principle of Least Effort*, Cambridge, Mass., 1949.
[248] See P. Guiraud, *Problèmes et méthodes de la statistique linguistique*, Dordrecht, 1959.
[249] P. 89.

CONCLUSION

THIS chronological survey of the various stages linguistic science has passed through since the beginning of the last century has enabled us to see how an ever-increasing amount of data has become available and a scientific method conforming to the strictest criteria has been worked out. But throughout this development that has apparently gone harmoniously and steadily forward, how many accidents and clashes there have been! Founded on a romantic illusion, that of getting back to the origins of mankind, linguistics was on the point of being assimilated in the mid-nineteenth century to the natural sciences, and its object, language, was treated as a living organism. Then came the myth of language considered as something social and supra-individual located in the collective consciousness of a linguistic community. Then, in the second half of the twentieth century, extreme structural positions made language, considered as a system of forms existing independently of its contingencies, into a supra-human metalinguistic entity. Quite recently hopes were still being expressed that, with the use of a logico-mathematical method, linguistics would return to the fold of the exact sciences. One illusion after another, from one generation to another—but these were nevertheless the driving forces behind ever deeper and ever more productive research.

Quite apart from these doctrinal exaggerations which are the extreme manifestations of a growing science that is always alive to new possibilities, linguistics has taken on an entirely new appearance in the last century and a half. Whereas last century the linguist was confronted with a mass of factual data, he now finds himself face to face with a structure, for it must be reiterated that structure is the mainspring of contemporary linguistics. Yesterday linguistics was a work of erudition; today it has become a science.

This clear-cut opposition between the two ways of looking at the study of language is the justification for the plan adopted in this book. In Part I we dealt with the nineteenth century and the growing awareness of linguistic realities, the classifying and arranging of a countless mass of facts, the formation of a sound scientific method; in Part III we dealt with our own period which is characterized by the acute desire to integrate the varying data provided by observation into a structure; between the two, in Part II, forming a hinge and sparking off the renewal of linguistics, there was Ferdinand de Saussure.

What of the future? For a science that is so young and so dynamic, the outlook must be bright. There are grounds for hope that new discoveries will provide food for thought (such as the decipherment of old documents or the recording of hitherto unknown tongues). Above all, we must look forward to new methods of analysis, of classification and of comparison. One need only think, to quote a single example, of all that remains to be done in the field of typology.

The human sciences are interpretative sciences, and a variety of interpretations are always possible; that is what makes the temptation so strong for a research worker to clutch at the methods of the natural sciences, or even at the possibility of mathematical certainty. But as a human science, linguistics must not fall into this trap. The constant renewing of hypotheses and the uncertainty of the conclusions reached are not in the least surprising. Is not the study of man a shifting terrain wherein there is always something new to be discovered?

Index of Names

Adelung, J. 7
Apostel, L. 76 n., 89
Aristotle 3, 10, 38, 73
Arnauld, A. 10
Aron, R. 72 n.
Ascoli, G. J. 40
Aulus Gellius 6

Bach, E. 81 n.
Bachelard, H. 51 n.
Bahner, W. 41 n.
Baldinger, K. 139 n.
Bally, Ch. 51, 62, 86 n., 87, 132,
    136, 137
Bartoli, M. 47 n., 104–105, 105 n.,
    112 and n.
Basilius, H. 29 n.
Baskin, W. 49 n., 52 n., 54 n.
Bastian, J. R. 93 n.
Baudouin de Courtenay, J. 65
Belardi, W. 110 n.
Benveniste, E. 51 n., 84 and n.,
    85–86, 91, 98 n., 115, 124, 127
    and n., 128, 131
Bérard, V. 9 n.
Bertoldi, V. 112
Bertoni, G. 104, 109 n.
Bloch, B. 80, 116, 134
Bloch, J. 31 n.
Bloomfield, L. 18 n., 83, 98, 116
Bolelli, T. 109
Bonfante, G. 104 n., 112, 122 n.
Bopp, F. 12–15, 16, 24, 26, 34,
    37, 58, 115
Bréal, M. 19, 34, 37–39, 133,
    139 n.
Bredsdorff, J. H. 13

Brøndal, V. 73, 74
Brugmann, K. 31, 35, 39, 41, 100,
    115
Brunot, F. 92
Butler, J. 25 n.
Buyssens, E. 25 n., 63 n., 72 n.,
    83, 86 n., 96 n.

Calepino, A. 6
Cantineau, J. 65 n., 70 n., 80 n.,
    122 n.
Carnap, R. 134
Carney, E. vii n.
Carroll, J. B. 78 n.
Cassirer, E. 134
Chomsky, N. 54 n., 81
Cœurdoux 11
Cohen, M. 93 n., 97, 119, 121
Condillac, E. de 10
Conway, R. S. 31 n.
Coseriu, E. 82 n., 88, 90
Croce, B. ix, 100–106, 101 n.,
    105 n., 110, 128 n., 132
Cuny, A. 31 n., 122 n.

Dall'Igna Rodrigues, A. 82 n.
Dante 5, 109
Darwin, C. 16, 43
d'Aubignac 9 n.
Dauzat, A. 28 n., 41 n.
Delacroix, H. 92, 117
Delbrück, B. 31, 39
de Mauro, T. 110 n.
Descartes, R. 10, 45, 46
de Stefano, A. 24 n.
Devoto, G. 104 n., 106, 108, 112
    and n., 122 n.

Index of Subjects

Accent 120
Acoustic gestures 25; image 52
Acoustics and phonetics 120
Adstratum 113; see also Loan words
Adyghe 67
Aesthetics 2, 70, 100–111, 128
Affective elements of language 62, 73 n., 132, 136; see also Expressive variants
Affinity 51 n., 104 n., 122
Affix 18, 125, 129
Affixal type 125
African languages 8, 121, 124
Agglutinating 18 n.
Agglutinative languages 18–23; technique 129–130
Albanian 42, 126
Alexandrian grammarians 4, 140
Algonkin 129
Alternation, of sonants 33; positive/negative 33, 69; vocalic 21, 32–33, 57, 67, 69, 129; voiced/voiceless 69
American linguists 29–30, 80, 83–84, 98, 116–117, 123, 128–130, 134
Amerindian languages 7, 8, 27, 82, 116, 121, 123–129
Analogists 4
Analysis, diachronic 91
Analytic languages 28; 'synthesis' 129
Ancients and moderns, quarrel of 44
Anglo-Saxon 57
Animal communication 51 n.

Anomalists 4
Aperture 67
Applied linguistics 78 n., 81, 119
Arabic 12, 46, 125, 129
Arbitrary nature of the sign 3, 50–53, 65 n., 85–87, 109
Archaic, languages considered as 32
Archaisms 113–114
Archiphoneme 68 n.
Arctic zone 126
Areal theory 113
Areas of extension 40
Armenian 4, 13, 42, 114
Article 74
Artificial languages 99
Aryan 17; see also Indo-Iranian
Aryo-Greco-Italo-Celtic 17
Asiatic Society of Calcutta 11
Aspect 4
Associations, auditory 25
Associative field 136; relationships 136
Atlantic zone 126
Atlas, linguistic 40
Attic 45
Audio-visual techniques 120
Auditory associations 25
Avestan 41, 46
Axes 56–57

Babel, Tower of 5
Balkan zone 126
Baltic languages 13, 16, 17, 42
Balto-Slavic 17, 41
Bantu 22 n., 125
Barbarian languages 2–4

147